THE SHEEP DOG:
ITS WORK AND TRAINING

Also by Edward Hart:

The Golden Guinea Book of
Heavy Horses Past and Present

Northcountry Farm Animals

Shepherds' Crooks and Walking Sticks (with David Grant)

THE SHEEP DOG:
ITS WORK AND TRAINING

TIM LONGTON
and
EDWARD HART

DAVID & CHARLES
NEWTON ABBOT LONDON
NORTH POMFRET (VT)

ISBN 0 7153 7149 5

First published 1976
Second impression 1976
Third impression 1977
Fourth impression 1978

Library of Congress Catalog Card Number 76-4370

© Tim Longton and Edward Hart 1976

Printed in Great Britain
by Redwood Burn Limited, Trowbridge and Esher
for David & Charles (Publishers) Limited
Brunel House Newton Abbot Devon

Published in the United States of America
by David & Charles Inc
North Pomfret Vermont 05053 USA

To Spy, Snip, Nell and Ken
and their successors Roy and Cap
—all great dogs

Tim Longton is a Lancashire hill farmer who has won the English National Farmers' Championship five times. He began his trials career in 1950 when he won the Shepherds' Championship with Nell. In 1966 he gained the ISDS Supreme award at Chester with Ken, the famous dog with which he has twice won the coveted Longshaw, Derbyshire, trials. His dogs Roy and Cap have won the National brace competition three times since 1973. In this book Tim Longton talks to Edward Hart, an agricultural journalist who formerly farmed sheep in a Yorkshire dale.

CONTENTS

page

List of Illustrations 9

Foreword by Lt Col K. J. Price, DSO, MC 11

Preface 13

1 Choosing a Dog 15

2 Management 25

3 Breeding 29

4 The Sheep Dog's Year 38

5 Commands 50

6 Training—First Stages 56

7 Training—Later Stages 64

8 Trials—Outrun, Fetch and Drive 77

9 Trials—Shed, Pen and Single 88

10 Judging 96

11 Obedience and Working Trials (*Audrey Wickham*) 105

12 The International Sheep Dog Society 112

Glossary 117

Bibliography 119

Acknowledgments 121

Index 123

LIST OF PLATES

page

Good Border collie head; correctly-set tail — 17

Ideal kennels; well-trained dog assisting in photography — 18

Cap in lambing field; keeping young dog off sheep — 35

Brace work in three stages — 36

Line of dogs holding flock of ewes; two dogs hold Scottish Blackfaces — 45

Roy with aggressive heifers; Border collie with bulls — 46

Winter scene in Scotland; working dog in Bowmont valley, Roxburgh — 47

Working a large flock of Welsh Mountain ewes; turning a flock of North Country Cheviots — 48

Tot Longton and Ken begin Longshaw trials; Tim Longton and Cap face trouble at Longshaw — 57

Three stages of Roy's successful Longshaw penning — 58

Friendly scene in the judging ring; examination for progressive retinal atrophy — 75

Shepherds' crooks; happy group of trialists — 76

FIGURES

page

Two typical trial courses   80, 81

All photographs by Edward Hart; line drawings by the Misses D. M. and E. M. Alderson

FOREWORD

"TRUST"   D.M ~ E.M.ALDERSON

My family has been intimately connected with sheep and sheep dogs for many generations. My grandfather organised the first-ever sheep dog trials here at Rhiwlas and the centenary trials were held here in 1973 only a few yards from the original site.

It is therefore with great pleasure that I write this Foreword and wish every success to Tim Longton's and Edward Hart's book on the Border collie. I am sure that everyone connected with sheep and sheep dogs will enjoy it and learn from it. Likewise, everyone who likes to watch sheep dog trials will get a lot more enjoyment from them if they read this book and learn all about the finer points.

I wish that every ordinary farmer who owns a sheep dog could be persuaded to read this book, especially the chapter on management, and learn to feed his dogs properly. I fear there are still far too many sheep dogs kept in dark, cramped quarters and fed on a totally inadequate diet of flaked maize and bread crusts. The sheep dog is such a willing and uncomplaining worker and without him the farmer could not even begin to look after his sheep. He should therefore show his thanks by giving his dog a proper diet and plenty of affection.

I am now going to make one suggestion for the sheep dog trials of the future. A tremendous advance has recently been made in the design of sheep pens or yards. Today one man and his dog can do all sorts of routine jobs with the flock that previously required the employment of several men. With the present scarcity of labour it is becoming more and more important to have a dog who excels at working sheep round the yards. I would like to see one of the larger trials organise a pen and a drafting race through which the sheep have to be driven and shedded, instead of the conventional method of shedding in the open inside the sawdust circle.

Finally let me say how much I have enjoyed reading this book and how much I have learnt from it. I must also congratulate Miss Audrey Wickham for her excellent chapter on obedience trials and the Misses D. M. and E. M. Alderson for their really splendid line drawings.

RHIWLAS   LT COL K. J. PRICE
BALA   DSO, MC
NORTH WALES

PREFACE

Sheep dogs are indispensable to sheep management. There are well over one thousand million sheep in the world, and one-third of this vast total is kept in countries where the Border collie is the chief work dog. Anything that can be done to raise working standards will help the world food situation. Energy and man-hours are both wasted by badly bred, ill-trained dogs, and the prime purpose of this book is to avoid such waste.

The average Border collie in average hands can perform every expected duty among sheep, not forgetting its value for cattle. Both classes of stock know immediately when the dog is absent, or if it is of no use. There are expensively mechanised farms where, to move bullocks from one field to another or bring sheep into the yards, involves turning out the entire farm staff. A good sheep dog could do the whole job more easily and economically. Our aim is to provide a straightforward means of improving the situation. The stimulus and excitement of the trials field is not neglected, and we are very appreciative of the value of obedience training among non-working dogs. Stray and untrained dogs

13

PREFACE

constitute a major threat to our livestock industries, and bringing all dogs to basic obedience-levels not only makes them happier, but is a positive step towards more food and less waste of time and energy.

CHOOSING A DOG

D·M· & E·H·ALDERSON
1975'.

Naebody wad sell a gude dowg, and naebody wad buy an ill yin.

A Border shepherd, quoted by Dr 'Rab' Brown (1810)
in Sidney Moorhouse: *British Sheepdog*

'Apart from his work, there is not much to be said about the Border collie,' explained Britain's leading canine authority, A. Croxton Smith. How right he is. Border collies vary in size; they may be black, black and white, or tricolour including tan, merle or red. They are short-backed, narrow in the chest, strong in the loin, with hocks and stifles well bent. Shepherds prefer broad 'hare' feet, well covered, either pricked or semi-erect ears and a coat either smooth or long. The Border collie's conformation enables him to do his best with the least effort. First appearances count. Generally speaking, if you don't like a dog the moment your eyes light on it, the chances are that you never will. One exception was when Mr Reid, then secretary of the

International Sheep Dog Society, sent my father a dog from Scotland. I well remember my father's great disappointment when he came home after meeting the collie at the railway station. A rough-looking, beardie-coated animal, my father did not like the dog's appearance at all. Yet when he took it to work next day, he was just as pleased, and ran it for many years.

There are many advantages in buying a pup. It should be at least six and preferably eight weeks old. Bought at this stage, the pup will spend its formative months with you. Provided the pups are all physically sound, there is no way of distinguishing their potential at this stage. You might just as well leave the choice to someone else, as the various theories propounded, such as the one the bitch picks up first to carry back to the nest, or the one that comes forward to greet you, do not stand scrutiny. If you want a certain colour, well and good, but otherwise leave it to chance. Cap, who was fourth in the Supreme at two years old, was the last of a litter from which others had taken their choice, and Nell, my first dog to win a National award, was the wreckling from a litter of nine!

Eyes should preferably be dark and set squarely to the front, not squinting into the middle. Ears should not flop down, but stand squarely at the corners of the head. See that the jaw is not overshot (the lower jaw not protruding as far forward as the upper); this is vital if you might breed from the pup at some time, though it matters less in a work dog. There is little sense in buying a pup with such a fault, however. Hind legs should not be 'nipped', or pointing inwards at the hocks, neither should the hocks be set so low down that they cause the pup to walk on the back of its pads, though this fault is more likely in older dogs.

The tail is important. It must not curl sideways when viewed from behind. It is the dog's rudder, and in my experience dogs with badly set tails often have poor heads, and not enough brains. A badly set tail does not fold down in line with the hind legs, but projects from the body, allowing daylight between hocks and tail. When a dog with this type of tail is approaching its sheep the tail lifts. This looks bad, and may indicate a weak dog. A

16

Plate 1 Tim Longton's Cap, showing good Border collie head of the 'box-type', with squarely-dropping forehead, placid eye and jaws meeting correctly.
Plate 2 A correctly set tail. A Border collie's tail should follow the line of the spine and curve neatly down behind the hind legs. A high-set tail which flops up and down when the dog runs is a fault. Smut, shown here is only five months old.

Plate 3 Housing that sheep dogs deserve. Though kennels like these are seldom built today, the principle of house, outside run and a view of what is going on holds good.

Plate 4 A well-trained collie helps photography. Normally it would not be shown in the photo, but would be lying down in front of the sheep, then moving rapidly on command to bring the sheeps' ears forward by attracting their attention.

well set tail, on the other hand, looks part of the dog. It follows the curve of the hind legs, and drops tight on to the hocks. If the tail is properly set on there should be no movement from it when the dog is running.

The head itself should have a level top which drops squarely to the top of the jaw. The pup should look as though it is proud of itself when walking, as should a ram.

In a well bred litter, the probability is that no pup will have any of these hereditary defects, which is why picking a pup is a matter of chance. You may, of course, theorise as much as you like about the litter beforehand. It cannot be stressed too strongly that if you want a work dog both parents should be work dogs, not merely the winners of small trials. Don't go for a certain strain just because everyone else does. (*See Chapter 3.*) If you seek a work dog and not a future sire or dam, pedigree is of small account. There are poor performers in litters of distin-guished lineage, and good ones from stock of no great pedigree. Don't pay fancy prices because the great-grandsire won the International through being expertly handled! Buyers are often very disappointed in pups bred with half-a-dozen trials-winning names in their pedigrees. Far better be pleased with a dog from ordinary parents, of whom no great prowess is claimed. To buy a pup by my Roy out of a Wiston Cap bitch, and to expect some-thing fabulous as a matter of course, is seeking disappointment.

Black-and-white is the fashionable colour. One buyer sought a pup with a certain amount of tan, simply because his old dog had patches of that shade. This is as good a reason as any other for preferences, the only colour to avoid being too much white. If sheep are not used to a light-coloured dog they will probably stop to look at it, or even go towards it. A very white dog has to be much better than a darker one to be equally useful with sheep.

An older dog may be bought fully broken or just starting to work. If the former, the first point is the way it gathers. You cannot do anything with the sheep until you have got them where you want them. Note whether the dog gathers those sheep that the handler intended, whether it runs very wide and is inclined to waste time, or whether it goes straight up the middle! A dog that runs past the sheep it is gathering is better than one that does not go far enough. I like to see the sheep brought on after the gather by the dog's unaided work, ie not under the whistle. You may then assess that dog's own potential, and not its reaction to an expert handler. If only a few sheep are being fetched, the dog should not run from side to side too much, as this indicates weakness and turning away. If it has a big mob under command, however, it must run from side to side and work at the corners, otherwise each sheep will take its own line, grazing *en route*.

The dog should not stand transfixed, with too much 'eye'. This is as big a detriment as too little. ('Eye' is the amount of concentration on the sheep that the dog shows.) Ideally it should be just enough that it will move freely. A certain amount is all right for inducing obedience, but too much is a great time-waster. Instead of working its sheep, the collie stands or lies, simply staring at them, often impervious to commands to 'walk up'. A dog that has little 'eye' is easier to break and easier to control, and it takes less out of itself as it works more easily. Sheep accept the collie with only a little 'eye', when they would be frightened by a strong 'eye'. In close work such as shedding, a strong-eyed dog is a nuisance. For this task it is essential that sheep move slightly apart, which they will do for a relaxed, casual type of dog, whereas they tend to hang together for safety against a strong 'eye'. Breeders have realised all this, and there are not so many strong-eyed dogs as there were twenty years ago.

Temperament is not easy to assess on first sight. A dog may be timid with people, yet full of courage against big beef cows. I recently sold Bett, out of Harry Huddleston's supreme champion Bett, and sired by Ken. The little dog is a terrific worker, but she is very shy of people, especially ladies. She works wonderfully at home, but trembles at the sight of crowds when taken to a trial. When the buyer called, Bett would not make friends or approach the strange people, yet while she was working stock in the yard she dashed close to them as though they were not there. Her new owner needed a lambing dog urgently; he works a farm single-handed where three full-time men formerly ran the place, another example of the importance of well-trained Border collies to a diminishing farm staff.

Unless you have no cattle on your farm, don't buy a dog that will not work both sheep and cattle. Such an animal is a great nuisance. If it won't work cattle this is frequently because it is frightened of them, and it will skulk about in a field where both classes of stock are grazing, as they frequently are. The sheep-only dog wastes a lot of time steering clear of the hoofs of cattle, whereas all our hints on training are designed to save time. Occasionally one hears of nasty accidents where a valuable dog is kicked by a cow, but in general little harm occurs. Dogs may react quite differently to the two classes of stock. Ken was one of my best with cattle, absolutely fearless and never giving ground, yet with sheep he would press very patiently without jumping in. In fact, on the final day at the 1966 International Trials at Littleton, Cheshire, he gained his place with his steadiness. We had only two sheep left to shed, and I became impatient and moved forward to part a sheep that was in the act of changing its mind. Ken remained steady as a rock, quite obviously knowing it couldn't be done. Yet that same dog would challenge the fiercest cow without flinching.

When buying a mature dog it is absolutely essential to spend time with the vendor, learning his code of commands. One whistle may sound almost the same as another to our ear and yet to the dog be entirely different; and if the whistle sounds different, it is different. Practice time and again until you are sure you have got it right. A word to the vendor here: do not let your buyer take the dog until he has thoroughly mastered the commands, otherwise you are simply storing up trouble for all three parties, and being especially unfair to the dog. Voice commands are easier to pass on than whistles, 'Way to me' offering less chance of confusion than a half tone on a whistle, but remember also that dog men are often hill men, and they stick to their dialects. Scotsmen have more twang than men south of the Border, and a command from a Scot may sound like a foreign language to a dog trained on the Pennines or the Welsh mountains!

If the collie you buy is registered, notification must be given to the International Sheep Dog Society (*see Chapter 12*). Possibly you will take the dog straight home with you after seeing it run, but in many instances a dog or pup is bought unseen or has to stay with its vendor for a while for a variety of reasons. For dispatch by train a wooden box with a metal grille or a wire or slatted top is needed. Cardboard boxes should not be used, as they may collapse under pressure. Paper lining in the base is simplest and cheapest, and pups seem to prefer it to other materials.

There is now an important international trade in British-bred Border collies. Veterinary certificates and certain innoculations are required by Australia, Canada and America, but check with the Ministry of Agriculture's Animal Health Division for exact details of the country concerned. Specialist housing is needed, and is generally provided. Glen went to Australia by air; we took him to Manchester Airport where he went into a box bought from the exporting company. Flying to London, he was cared for by the RSPCA, flying to Australia next day.

This brings me to a very important point when buying an older dog. You may be delighted with its performance under the vendor's handling in accustomed surroundings, but it is difficult to tell whether the dog will settle in its new home with its new master. Only time will tell. One of my favourite sayings is, 'There's a dog for the man, and a man for the dog.' The first essential is patience. You simply must give the dog time to become accustomed to you. I heard of an experienced horse-breaker who put his young horses into loose-boxes and did absolutely nothing with them for a full fortnight apart from handling them and gaining their confidence. This seems a good principle to apply to greeting a new dog.

Never pay fancy prices for a pup. You have no guarantee that the best-bred pup will turn out suitable, and there are any amount of pups at £12 to £20. For an older dog, the question is entirely different. Capabilities are already apparent. You know what you are getting, and the only question is the length of time the dog will take to settle down. There is little point in considering a trained dog under £75, though we still have farmers who think they have a right to a willing slave for £30 to £40. Then, when they get it, they shut it up and forget about it until it is needed and then wonder why it doesn't immediately perform well, like a tractor. Considering the scores of hours put into bringing out a competent work dog, even prices well into three figures are little enough recompense. I must say that these points are better appreciated than they were a few years ago.

Obviously there are cash limits to what a man can pay for a dog, but the fact is that hill sheep-farming would be impossible without good Border collies, and lowland sheep-farming more difficult. I would never dream of doing any job among sheep, including lambing, without a dog at my side. Those lowland farmers who say 'Don't have a dog anywhere near the sheep at lambing' merely demonstrate their own and their shepherds' incapacity at dog training and handling.

On the worth of the dog in the hills, Ralph Fleesh wrote in 1910:

> Were twenty picked athletes sent out in the early morning to accomplish the work of collecting and 'bughting', the chances are that they would not reach the fold till the shades of night were falling, and they might fail altogether. Sheep soon learn to outwit man—they seldom challenge the prowess of a thoroughly trained Collie. It thus becomes clear what Hogg, for instance, points out, that but for the Collie sheep-farming would be an almost impossible industry. And all the wages the faithful fellow asks are home-grown meals, a straw bed, and a little kindness!

When selling a dog, ascertain the type the buyer wants. Run your dog accordingly. If he wants a wide runner, set off your dog to give a wide sweep, and if he wants a tight runner, direct the dog in that fashion. You are not trying to deceive when bringing out the appropriate qualities. Your buyer may seek a forceful dog with a bit of dash, or he may want one that keeps well off the sheep. As the seller, it is up to you to show what is required.

2

MANAGEMENT

All great dogs, like all great men, work not because they have to, but because they want to. Action is their chief medium of happiness.

Ralph Fleesh (1910)

A whole book could be written on nutrition and the Border collie. Fortunately we can leave this to others, and confine ourselves to a few simple rules. There is now a wide range of proprietary foods available, blended by men who understand the science of nutrition and who, in the brand that I use at any rate, really care about dogs. They are 'dog men', and study world markets and buy commodities to make up their rations in a way no individual can hope to match. No concentrate food is cheap now, but proprietary brands have to be competitive. The food should be guaranteed to contain a large number of different ingredients. (*See Chapter 3.*) Dogs function better when properly fed.

Manufacturers supply instructions on quantities. These can only be approximate for the average dog. Certainly no hard-and-fast rule can be applied. The dog's back should be the criterion. Learn the difference between fit and fat. A working dog should be fit but not fat, a state easier to advocate than to achieve. Dogs, like people, differ. Some keep their condition on very little, some easily become fat, others do not put on flesh however you feed them.

I hesitate to stress that over-feeding is possible, because I feel so grieved to see dogs at work which are manifestly underfed. The poor things get neither sufficient amounts nor the proper ingredients; they work their hearts out for an ungrateful master who does not give them enough to replace all the energy they use.

With certain proprietary brands of dog food it is essential to supply clean water. This is clearly stated, and to neglect to do so is both harmful and cruel. I feed a wet mash and don't give water separately, but water may be needed in hot weather. Dogs have their preferences also. When I bought Snip, one of my early National runners, from Mr Jolly, he said, 'Don't watch her eat. She's a finicky feeder.' And so it proved. Put Snip's food out and remain in the place, and she would not look at it. I think she would have starved first. Go quietly away, and a few minutes later Snip would slink out and delicately clean her dish. You couldn't feed that dog according to a chart, but she was one of the best. Spy, Ken's mother, had to be rationed severely, or she grew as fat as a pig. Ken himself was a normal feeder. Little Nell would get too fat if not at work, but after a fortnight's routine running was back in hard condition. Recently I got a pup from Scotland, and it was such a bad feeder that I almost lost it. It was kennelled with another pup of good appetite, and I left a large lump of raw meat in the building, and this saved the situation.

A dog that drinks great quantities of water should be avoided. This becomes a habit. On a hot day the dog will leave you to find water, then drink so much that it can't work. Do not tolerate such an animal.

A daily feed is sufficient for a mature dog, given each evening after work. At three weeks puppies should be drinking or 'lap-

26

ping', and are helped by cow's milk or proprietary puppy milk-substitute three times a day. If you don't feed so often, the bitch may not leave any for the pups. Don't begrudge her any; she has a big job with a large litter. I use calf milk-substitute, but only because it is available on the farm and has to be mixed anyway. At five weeks introduce a little hard feed, either natural dog-food or special puppy-mix. The bitch's milk is usually drying up at this stage, and weaning should be done gradually. From five weeks take the dam out for increasing periods during the day-time, until she only returns to her litter at night. If she still has a lot of milk, the pups may as well have it. Rubbing the teats with vinegar or a short period of fasting are effective methods of drying up the supply. Finally take the bitch away altogether, leaving the litter in accustomed surroundings.

Worm the pups at five weeks, at three months and at six months. Remember to use pup wormer, not old dog wormer. Mature dogs suffer chiefly from tapeworms, and should be wormed every year, or when symptoms show. Pups are very susceptible to lice, a condition associated with uncleanliness and poor feeding. Proprietary treatment against lice should be carried out at six weeks, a process which cleans up the coat generally. Bedding should be changed, as dirty bedding encourages lice.

Until they are six months old, pups should be fed milk and a proprietary compound three times a day. If you use these correct mixtures you don't have to bother about proteins, minerals or vitamins. From six to nine months feeding may be reduced to twice daily, and from then on the dog is classed as mature, and fed accordingly. There is no precise scale of feeding; keep the young dogs fit and growing, then you know you are on the right lines.

Puppies should be innoculated soon after weaning. A multiple vaccine is available, giving protection against distemper, hard pad, viral hepatitis (a disease of the liver) and leptospirosis (a disease of the kidneys). Boosters should be given as recommended. Remember that the first booster is given a fortnight after the first injection, and that two weeks later immunity has reached its height. After this time the dog can mix with other dogs to advantage, at places like sheep dog trials, and its immunity will be strengthened by so doing. A veterinary certificate is given to dogs that have had approved vaccinations, and this certificate should accompany the dog if it is sold.

A dog house should be free from draughts and should have a dry bed and ample fresh air and light. These simple criteria are by no means always met in Britain. Visitors to New Zealand report that proper dog accommodation is available on most farms, with both a kennel and an outside run. Rarely are chains used. Only too often I have seen dogs in Britain tied up at the end of a disused byre for days on end.

A little thought and effort can convert most existing buildings into satisfactory kennels. Concrete floors are not advisable. They remain wet from urine, and may lead to sore feet. Wood is far better, both for pen and run floor. A pen 6ft by 10ft and a house 6ft square will hold two dogs comfortably. A bench 6in to 1ft high should be fitted to either side of the house, with a board across the front and 3in higher, to keep bedding in place. The house roof must be weatherproof, and may or may not extend over the pen. Open sheds with snug kennels inside are quite satisfactory.

The pen is especially valuable for a young dog. It sees what is happening in the world outside, and is less nervous and silly on release. It learns to respect vehicles coming and going; a farmyard is a very dangerous place for puppies and young children alike.

3
BREEDING

*A good Collie, like a good horse, cannot be a bad colour. The
sense of hearing is marvellously acute in this breed, the semi-
erect ears of the true Collie apparently lending themselves by
their shape to the conveyance of sound; whilst the peculiar
swinging gait of Collie, which to some degree resembles the
skulking trot of his reputed ancestor the wolf, is a feature of
the variety.*

Standard Cyclopaedia of Modern Agriculture

Always remember a phrase from the constitution of the International Sheep Dog Society when deciding on matings: 'The
objects of the Society shall be to . . . secure the better management of stock by improving the Shepherd's Dog.' That is, or
should be, your object. The aim is not to breed a neat dog that
can trip round a small trials field with three sheep in front of it
and edge them in the required direction by keeping well off them.
Never depart from the ideal of the normal working dog—one

29

that can cope with large flocks, and with belligerent cows as well as sheep. Since most dogs go to work and never see a trials field, their needs must be fully borne in mind by the breeder.

Ideally a bitch should be over two years old before mating. This is on account of progressive retinal atrophy, examination for which may be inconclusive before two years old. Dr Keith Barnett and his colleagues at the School of Veterinary Medicine, Cambridge University, undertake these tests at various centres including all National and International trials. If both sire and dam are clear of progressive retinal atrophy, the chances are that the offspring will be free from this condition, which at one time threatened the breed. When your bitch first comes on heat at about a year old she is still immature. Wait a further year, and you are far more certain about the material you are moulding.

Some bitches come in season twice a year, some only once. Though the spring is the most likely time, they may come on in any month. Once heats have started, they should recur every five or six months in a normal bitch, but many bitches are not normal in this respect. The bitch will show blood for some ten days before the heat proper, but you must watch carefully around the expected time, for the symptoms are easy to miss. Mating may be possible five or seven days after the onset of blood, but bitches vary in this also. If a bitch will stand for service she should be mated, otherwise the vital time may be missed. This advice goes against others' experience in mating late in the heat period, when higher conception rates are claimed. As an example of how easy it is to delay mating too long, Bob Fraser brought his Betty here for mating with Cap one Wednesday after an English National. On Thursday the bitch was tried and would not stand; on Friday she was lined; on Saturday I was away all day and did not bother with Betty, who on Sunday would have nothing whatever to do with the dog. A bitch may be served two days in succession, but if the dog is being used a lot this policy is not fair to the owners of other bitches.

After lining, the bitch must be kept away from all other dogs until heat has finished completely, but if she is still in season a week after mating she should definitely be tried again. If sent away for mating, she should be put in a crate. Payment for service is usually at time of mating and varies between about £12 and £20 for the best dogs.

There are a few queer folk in the sheep dog world as in every other walk of life. One told me his bitch had not held to my Ken, and therefore he had nothing to pay. Shortly afterwards a neighbour told me what a grand pup of Ken's he had got from the same bitch! When I told him the circumstances he went off to threaten the bitch's owner, otherwise his pup would not be eligible for registration, and a mating fee arrived shortly afterwards!

After mating and the end of heat, the Border collie bitch may be worked much as usual. When halfway in pup, ie after about a month, she should be wormed. For feeding, use special proprietary rations for in-pup bitches, and choose one that guarantees a large number of ingredients. The brand we use works out slightly dearer per lb, but is cheaper over the vital period concerned, and gives better results than the flaked maize and fish meal we once used. It is no use expecting good pups out of a dam in poor condition.

The bitch may be worked right up to whelping, provided that she is accustomed to it. Use common sense. If the bitch is so heavy that she becomes distressed, then obviously she needs to take life easier; but a certain amount of normal work helps keep her in the correct condition. My brother once won a Claughton trial with a bitch that came home and pupped that night!

Introduce your bitch to her whelping quarters a full week before the expected date, to give her a chance to accustom herself to her new surroundings. If you don't, she may pup in various corners before deciding which she likes best. Give her plenty of dry bedding; I use clean straw. Don't chain her up, and in winter see that she is warm enough. A lamp may be necessary in severe weather. We don't want to encourage mollycoddling, but we do want to give the pups a chance. The building should have no ledge over which a pup might drop.

As whelping approaches, only the person to whom the bitch is accustomed should inspect her. Don't take strangers in. When the pups start arriving leave the bitch to herself if all is quiet. If pups are strewn about in various places then you must gather them together, but this rarely happens.

Apart from ascertaining the size of the litter, there is little to be done to the pups. With a large litter even more attention must be paid to the dam's feeding, but if the pups sleep most of the time then all is well. If they are constantly whimpering something is wrong, and they are very probably not getting enough milk. Proprietary brands of pup milk are now available, and are a great help. If your bitch has no milk at all then the pups must be fed at midnight and 3.00am, so it is a wearing task until they are three weeks old, when they should be able to drink. Artificial feeding has a far greater chance of success if introduced in time, for if the pups become weak they have great difficulty in sucking an artificial teat.

The dam requires plenty of liquids and you must ensure that fresh clean water is always available. Some milk is good, but too much will cause scour. With a large litter she may lose flesh whatever you do, but give her as much well-balanced food as she will take. Worm the pups at five weeks old; it is preferable to worm early rather than let the pups get down in condition through worms. You must of course use a pup wormer, not an adult type. Pups are troubled by roundworms only.

If all conversations about breeding sheep dogs had been recorded, they would take a very long time to play back. Yet how much depends on the strain, and how much on the man? The handler can only bring out what is already there, but a vast number of dogs work at well below their full potential simply through poor, slipshod training methods, and the most carefully thought out breeding plan is no recipe for producing an accomplished worker.

Some breeders are like a dog with a strong 'eye'. They become transfixed by names in the pedigree, delving right back to the breed's origins. This is all very well, but do they produce outstanding Border collies as a result? The answer is that they don't. You are more likely to find an outstanding dog in a litter from registered parents with winning names in their pedigrees, but there is no certainty that this will be so. Because every Tom, Dick and Harry takes his bitches to a certain dog, that is no reason for you to do the same. If you are a stud breeder, you may want a particular line of blood in your Border collies, in which case it is up to you to arrange matters, but the pups will still be only as good as the man that has them.

One of the dangers of going to a trials-winning dog, or any dog belonging to another, is that you don't really know that dog. You only see it working under a certain set of conditions. You don't know what it was like during training; whether it was amenable, needed very careful handling, or almost had to have sense knocked into it. I am concerned lest the Border collie becomes too 'soft' (*see Glossary*), but how to rectify the situation is another matter. My dog Roy is rather on the 'soft' side; he doesn't like to be told off if things go wrong. Yet his son, Vic, is so 'hard' that he won't take notice of anything I say. We are breeding for brains, and for conformation to the extent of sound physical characteristics. We must also breed for character, by which I mean placid nature, a temperament that will withstand discipline and do what it is told to the letter without going 'soft'.

Half the trouble is that these 'soft', tender dogs tend to win small trials on good sheep. People see their neat working and think, 'I must have a pup from her,' or, 'I must take my bitch to him.' Then they are frequently disappointed because they don't breed real work dogs. Beware of dogs that win trials on good sheep, but can't cope with difficult ones.

Nothing makes me more mad than these 'soft' dogs, yet they are the very ones to whom most harm is done by any loss of temper. Always remember that ill-feeling immediately communicates itself in this partnership between dog and man. This is another reason why any dog is only as good as the man that has it. Dogs can be sharp-tempered too. When Nell was having a rough passage, her tail end gave a little sideways flick, and I

33

learned to identify this signal and give her a hand. When I got annoyed with the situation, as I did more often when I had her twenty-five years ago, she would hang back and give me a certain look out of her eye corners as if she was telling me to cool off a little. We had a five-acre meadow, full of lambing sheep, and I could stand at the bottom and send Nell off. 'In' and 'Back' were her direction commands, and she would thus arrive at a certain sheep, work it and its lamb to the wall, and stand over it while it suckled. I would give a lot for another Nell.

A distinct danger threatens the Border collie if a very few blood lines permeate the breed too thoroughly. That redoubtable Scottish handler John Richardson is a great friend of mine, and his dog Wiston Cap is among the greatest in history, winning the Supreme at eighteen months old. I have used Wiston Cap myself, but he has sired so many hundreds of pups in the past ten years that another outstanding strain is sorely needed. The girls in the International Sheep Dog Society office never look up Wiston Cap's number; they know it by heart! Let me make it perfectly clear that I am not belittling this dog in any way; I am simply stressing the dangers of too close breeding which must surely follow excessive use of one sire, however good and sound he is.

The words of the first Clydesdale Horse Society Secretary, Thomas Dykes, in 1880 are worth recalling.

Occasionally an argument crops up on the subject of 'in-breeding', and a great amount of irrelevant matter appears. It has, indeed, been used as an argument against stud books. Stud books are merely the record books of experience with certain well-defined materials, and no argument can be used against them in any shape or form. In-breeding is just as legitimate as out-breeding—a step in a certain direction. No move should be made by the breeder without some purpose in view, and if he breeds or crosses out he is understood to be working towards his object. Some few people adopt, unfortunately, the line of parallel arguments, and because Shorthorn Cattle have been most successfully in-bred, adopt the same principle in breeding Clydesdales. The objects are, however, entirely different. The spirit of the Shorthorn is

34

Plate 5 Cap at work in the lambing field. A dog concentrating on the ewe arouses her maternal instincts and makes her more willing to take an orphan lamb.

Plate 6 Keeping a young dog off its sheep. Dot, featured in a TV training programme, is inclined to work too close, and Tim Longton is showing that it must only approach on command.

Plate 7 (top) Brace work. Roy and Cap holding Dalesbred ewes with twin lambs while those with singles are driven elsewhere.

Plate 8 (centre) Roy (on right) begins the separation process by driving off ewes with singles.

Plate 9 (below) Cap holds this bunch while the rest are pushed through a gate to new pastures. A stone wall is less dangerous to dogs and stock than barbed wire.

bred out of him, and he becomes a block of beef, just what is wanted. The spirit of the Clydesdale is one of his best characteristics, and the breeder must always keep this in view.

As with working horses, so with working dogs. Courage and character count for much. Horsemen of the older generation say that the Clydesdale was more sensible, easier to break, and less temperamental before the period of in-breeding. We have available the examples of many classes of stock over long periods. Border collies are bred for brains and character. They may be good looking, but that is a bonus, not an end in itself.

All breeders know the leading strains in the present Border collie. One of the greatest is Whitehope Nap, with whom J. M. Wilson won the International at Edinburgh in 1955. Len Greenwood's Moss has Whitehope Nap blood, as have many more. Gilchrist's Spot has founded another famous line, grandsons and granddaughters being especially promising. Alan Jones' Roy is among the best dogs ever bred in Wales, while Thomson MacKnight's Gael is the female ancestor of many good dogs on both sides of the Border. Llyr Evans' Bosworth Coon was a popular sire, and Bob Fraser's Mindrum strain has been founded for half a century. Bob believes in strong dogs that come in to their sheep—the Mindrum strain has no use for weaklings.

4

THE SHEEP DOG'S YEAR

There now came a development in the use of trained dogs for gathering and driving sheep. The origin of the association between the sheepdog and the flock is obscure. It was at least as old in the lowlands as the 'good barkable dog' of the medieval treatises. In Wales there are [in 1870] men living who can recollect seeing the natives dressed in running costume for the task of gathering the mountain . . . and going so fleet of foot as would outstrip a four-year-old mountain wether. Now the Highland Sheep Dog, introduced from Westmorland some years ago, has made the task a comparatively easy one.

R. Trow-Smith:
A History of British Livestock Husbandry (1700–1900)

The shepherd's year begins in autumn. This is a convenient time to start the Border collie's year, and to analyse the various tasks confronting it through the different seasons.

After tupping we herd our sheep to the top of the hill each day.

Then as the weather gets worse they can come lower down where the bottom grazing has been saved for them. Scotsmen 'rake' the hillside daily by driving the sheep up each evening. In either case a 'driving' dog is needed to drive the sheep away from the handler. The way to do this is discussed in Chapter 6. Sheep soon become accustomed to this routine; the dog trains them.

At certain times the dog works very hard indeed, for very long hours. At other seasons its services are scarcely needed, and it is during the latter periods that chances of neglect are greatest. The sheep dog is not a machine like a tractor, to be switched off and left until needed again. It has feelings, and a body in need of exercise. Hence out-of-season treatment is as necessary to successful dog handling as is care in spring and autumn, when activity is called for during most of the daylight hours.

The ewes must be gathered before tupping, and sorted into their different lots. The dog's part is mainly to round up or gather all the ewes in a field into a pen or yard, where they are sorted by hand. On the hill more expertise is needed for almost every operation, as the scale and nature of the ground is so different. A 'clean gather' must be achieved as nearly as possible, otherwise some ewes will be missing when the tups go out and their year's production will be lost.

The good hill dog makes a wide sweep of the boundary, an exercise simulated by the 'outrun' on a trials field. Once the sheep are moving they will join up with others, and when the flock is collected the dog's job is to bring them to the pens in a quiet and orderly manner. Then the dog is mainly a spectator as the shepherd decides which ewes will run with which tup, but it joins in to move sheep from one pen to another. The trek back to the various paddocks or parts of the hill begins. With well-shepherded sheep this is not a particularly arduous task compared with working young lambs; all the sheep are mature, and will have learnt to respect the dog.

Both shepherd and dog work hard at tupping time; it is the foundation of a successful lambing time. On the hill each lot of ewes is gathered daily around the male or males that run with them. Ewes wander away to graze, and if they are not gathered daily some may not have a chance of the tup. Hence man and dogs move from one lot to another, rounding up these stragglers and ensuring that the correct tups are present in each lot, not half a mile away among someone else's ewes. If the tups are caught to be fed, and raddled with bright colour on their chests to mark the ewes, the dog holds up the whole bunch while the shepherd catches the animal he requires.

The practice is similar, if simpler, on lowland farms. A trained sheep dog enables the shepherd to do his job of checking that the tups are present, that they are working satisfactorily, and that all ewes, including the younger and more nervous ones, are brought within range of the flock sire. Tupping lasts for five weeks, after which some 'chaser' rams may remain with the flock, but the vital daily routine is replaced by a check at longer intervals.

Sheep must be pressed uphill steadily by a dog under control. They must not be rushed, and the nearer lambing approaches the more this rule applies. The value of a steady dog that does not push too hard is illustrated by an experience I had in Lakeland. As patrol shepherd I was helping to gather a very steep hill face of the type that abounds there. I had with me a dog called Glen, run by my father in trials. An old horned ewe with half a fleece still on was trailing behind the others gaining the summit, her lamb by her side. Glen approached. The old ewe stopped, looked and stamped. Glen stopped also, intent. The ewe saw that he did not give way, and trundled up a few yards, when the process was repeated. All this time Glen was working four or five yards from her. I was calling and whistling to help send the other sheep ahead, while Glen stuck to his task, and eventually the old ewe and her lamb gained the top and joined the rest. The men looked at her in amazement. 'How did you get her up here?' they asked. 'Many a man has tried to bring that old girl in, and no one has done it yet!' (This was why she still had the half fleece on.) Every time a dog had pressed her, she had simply charged downhill with her lamb at her side, and the strongest dog in the world can do nothing in such circumstances. If Glen had not kept his distance, the same would have happened. Glen weighed up the situation and did this on his own account; I did not direct him after setting him on the particular ewe. There is something between dog and sheep that is outside human experience, for if Glen had shown the slightest lack of determination that ewe would have known and been at the foot of the hill in seconds, as she had done so many times before. If he had pressed too hard, she would have taken off just the same.

During winter the whole flock may be gathered, to draw out small and thin sheep, but generally the flock is best left alone as long as the weather is open. The dog's work is eased by the use of solid feed blocks distributed at strategic points on the hill, as these tend to keep sheep to particular areas as desired. Two weeks before lambing, all ewes may be gathered for their pre-lambing injections, and a well-trained Border collie becomes more important than ever; ewes heavily in lamb need the gentlest of treatment.

If winter storms come, the situation is changed. I believe that sheep have an instinct to avoid being caught by snow, and though they may sometimes be overblown and buried in deep drifts, I don't start to gather before a storm, though I do like to know where the sheep are. Other shepherds on other hills may not agree. If the worst does happen, and a really severe storm piles snow deep into any cover, a good Border collie is invaluable. Some dogs have a natural aptitude for tracking sheep in snow. Perhaps they simply have keener scent, for this is something that cannot be taught. They 'set' sheep in a drift, pointing like a gun dog. I cannot think of any cases where the particular aptitude is hereditary, but of course certain dogs pass most of their working lives without encountering really deep snow.

The best dog I ever had for this particular task of finding buried sheep was a 'beardie' collie called Ken—no relation to my supreme champion. Ken saved scores of sheep in the 1947 winter. He loved the job. 'Let's be off!' he would imply by dancing around on release from his kennel, and make straight away for the snow drifts. Generally a one-man dog, he didn't

41

bother about me at all under such conditions, but would go with anyone trying to find sheep. I was a shepherd at the time, and was out in the snow with my boss, who suddenly said: 'Ken's found one!' The dog lifted his nose in the air, then set off directly across a wide valley; you could trace his line in the snow, and it scarcely deviated a yard. The snow was so deep in the bottom that we walked round the tops to a mountain ash tree where Ken had stopped. When we arrived, the dog had dug a hole six feet deep in the drift, and had still not reached the sheep. I have often wondered what would have happened had he done so, and whether he would have torn the sheep in his efforts to free it.

Nell, with whom I won my first national championship, had an extremely keen nose—for rabbits! However, she had no snow to contend with. Nell was a great example of putting work first. On duty among sheep, she would not look at a rabbit, but once I had said, 'That'll do!'—the sheep dog's 'Stand easy!'—the next rabbit was hers.

We sincerely hope that all the snow has gone before gathering for lambing. This is a very particular job. I don't fear harm to the lamb itself; danger through hurrying sheep arises from the greater chances of triggering off 'staggers' (magnesium deficiency) and pneumonia. 'The quieter the better' is a rule for working sheep that cannot be repeated too often. Lambing time is the busiest period of all for shepherd and dog. It is a complete myth to say that no dog should be allowed in a lambing field (it is a reflection on those who believe it, for their dogs are not under command). During lambing, ewes and lambs must be constantly caught, and I had a bitch, Mist, which was exceptionally clever at this. I simply looked at either the ewe or the lamb I wanted, and Mist would drive it within reach of my crook in a flash. I did not even speak to her. In the first year I had to teach her to gather again, at the end of lambing time.

Dogs are invaluable for 'mothering-on'. If a ewe has to take a lamb not her own, her mothering instincts are roused if a dog is 'set' to watch her while the lamb sucks. She stamps at the dog and forgets that the lamb is strange. Often just one sheep must be cut out during lambing, and here you will find whether your dog is really on top of its job. Perhaps a lamb has to be taken home. The ewe's instinct is to dash back to the place where she lambed, but nine out of ten will follow the man carrying the lamb provided there is a dog behind it that walks steadily along without showing a sign of fear. Ken would come right through a flock with one sheep, and never look at the others. That reminds me of a story of a Lancashire hill farmer who wrapped a staple of wool round the horn of every sheep he wanted home, and afterwards sent in the dog, who returned with every marked sheep. As the field was 200 acres, and had 600 sheep in it, I keep an open mind!

An intelligent dog learns quickly that ewes with lambs are to be taken out of the lambing paddock, leaving behind those still to lamb. Conversely, if sheep without lambs are to be shifted, the well-bred Border collie soon appreciates the situation, and leaves those with lambs behind. Such jobs demand quietness all the time; they are done far more quickly if done quietly, rather than rushing around and upsetting the sheep.

By the time the hill lambs are back on the fell, lowland lambs may be ready for the butcher. Again, quietness when gathering is the watchword. Shearing is the next big job, for which an early start is a great advantage. A 4.00am start in hill country makes best use of cool conditions. The job is done in a quarter of the time with a quarter of the effort, being far easier on sheep and dogs. Some people gather at night ready for next morning, but sheep run downhill naturally at dawn, whereas in the evening their inclination is uphill. Lambs are well grown at this stage, and unless carefully dogged they dash off from their dams. Therefore steady progress is the watchword. A dog that dashes in among the flock causes much extra work by splitting lambs off, which causes the ewes to run back seeking them, wasting more time. If gathering is attempted during the heat of the summer day, sheep simply skulk into shade and dogs work like mad and get nowhere.

43

A well-authenticated story from a Lancashire farm describes what occurred one lunch time. As the men were trooping in they discussed gathering Daleside—a hill above the house—after the meal. Their dog was with them as they walked and talked. After dinner, the dog was missing—an unheard-of occurrence. They were debating what to do when someone looked up and saw all the sheep on Daleside approaching, with the dog in full command. Whether he had heard the name Daleside, as he must have done many times before, and set off on his own initiative, remains a mystery. Knowing sheep dog men, there is always the possibility that one had slipped out while the others were talking and arguing, and set the dog on his way!

Once in the yards, lambs are shed off before clipping. We always have a man and a dog in the pen, keeping the race full, with one man working the shedder. Dogs continue to help fill the pens and, if it is communal clipping day, to decide whether or not they like their neighbours' dogs.

After shearing, the ewes are let out into a handy paddock, where the lambs join them. If these are in reasonably small lots, so much the better. They are then left till the next day to sort themselves out and 'mother up'. A quiet dog is essential here. When checking to see that every lamb has found its dam, take the dog to the gate from which the sheep know they return to the hill. Walk slowly through them, and if you find a ewe with no lamb, take it down with the dog's help until you find a spare lamb. A wild dog is completely useless at this stage, as ewes and lambs will simply jumble together in front of it, and you cannot see which is which. The dog's task is made harder by the vogue for contract shearers, who demand large lots of sheep.

When the wool has grown a bit, the flock must be gathered again for dipping. A well trained yard dog helps the flow of sheep into the dipper pens. At this stage some of the lambs may be weaned or speaned, and the process of taking lambs off the ewes causes some of the hardest work of the dog's year. We used to take all ours to the fell end for weaning, and drive the lambs back home. Now we limit lambs to lots of about 100. If there are 400

44

Plate 10 Dalesbred ewes at Rooten Brook make no attempt to break the line of watchful dogs but go steadily to the yards for sorting and injecting. All four collies compete in trials – the young black-and-white Petra (extreme right) is just starting her nursery career.

Plate 11 Scottish Blackface ewes and lambs being held by two Border collies for inspection by National Sheep Association members on a Dumfriesshire hill farm.

Plate 12 Roy holds his ground under attack from an aggressive Angus/Friesian heifer. Border collies vary enormously in temperament, but a good one will tackle the hardest cattle yet put no more pressure on sheep than is necessary to move them.

Plate 13 This Border collie, Candy, is in daily use among the stud of bulls at the Milk Marketing Board's Whenby, York, centre. The manager rides among them on horseback, but never without his dogs as safeguard.

Plate *14* In the snows. Scottish Blackfaces held against the burn in a Perthshire glen. With winter may come the collies' greatest test.

Plate *15* An intelligent work dog in Bowmont valley, Roxburghshire: note the dog's steadiness and concentration. The sheep are two-shear Hill Cheviot rams; the breed originating on a neighbouring farm.

Plate 16 Larger flocks can only be worked by pressing in at the corners alternately as with these Welsh Mountain ewes on lower grazing.
Plate 17 On the turn. A Roxburghshire collie working a large flock of North Country Cheviots.

lambs in one mob it is almost impossible to drive them over an open space. They will go all right in a lane, but try them across country and they will jump on top of the dogs and do anything to return to their dams. With lambs the trick is to keep them going the right way with a dog pressing into the corners rather than dashing into the middle.

On one farm we had to dip all lambs against ticks at a few days old. Nell was suckling pups a fortnight old, so she had been left behind. She heard us trying to drive this lot along a rough bank where felled woodland and a landslide added to the hazards. I could hear her crying to be let out; a few minutes later she appeared, having gained the window. Two young lambs dashed uphill. Nell set off after them. She was fighting a losing battle, as the lambs split, and as soon as she had one on its way the other galloped madly in the other direction. I did not command her but, appreciating the position, Nell pushed one lamb in front of her and nosed it right in among the rest of the lambs. Then she returned for the other, which by now had escaped into a 200-acre field with 400 sheep in it. We continued our slow journey, and when we reached the far end there was Nell with a lamb pinned at the back of a gate. It was the lamb we wanted.

Once the lambs are taken off the ewes, dog work is lightened. The older sheep return to the fell or hill and need little attention until nearer sale time. Tups are to be watched at this period. A strong dog is required for them. Dogs know that they are tups and are different from ewes. The dog is more likely to be attacked, and some tups are very nasty indeed. My dog Cap is very hard on tups, yet merely firm with other sheep; he gears himself up immediately to overcome the stronger animals. Our tups tend to be well herded, often being called upon to provide practice, for which purpose I would be the last to say they are ideal.

5
COMMANDS

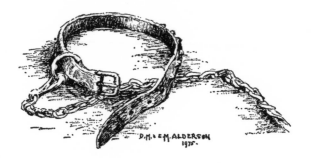

The training of the dog would seem to have been nearly the first art invented by man, the result of which was the conquest and peaceable possession of the earth and the various animals upon it.

R. W. Dickson: *Live Stock and Cattle*
(early nineteenth century)

The purpose of commands is to get a dog into any given position, relative to the sheep and the handler. It is not only what you say or whistle—it's the way that you do it. At one time a man ran all his dogs on the same set of whistles. If he had several dogs, and worked them together, he had to call the requisite name before giving the command. That method began to go out some forty years ago, and today the majority of handlers running brace (two dogs) have a separate code of commands for each.

Should you whistle or shout? Some handlers find whistling a very difficult art, even using an artificial whistle. Bosworth Coon won many a trial for Llyr Evans on voice alone. The arms should not be used much. If I want to redirect a dog to a new lot of sheep, I may point with my arm, but if a dog hasn't been taught to respond to sound properly, you have no right to expect it to respond to semaphore. It is rather like a bowls player leaning his body to get his wood nearer the jack after delivery; it's already too late!

Scotsmen are more inclined to talk to their dogs, Welshmen whistle, and English handlers fall somewhere in between. One American used a megaphone at the World Trials! If you know nothing about commands, go to a trial and listen. Note each handler's set of commands, as judged—hopefully—by the dog's reaction. Decide which is easiest for you.

Whistles performed easily by one handler are difficult for another, so practise the different combinations thoroughly at home before making up your mind. You will use them a lot, and often in difficult situations; they must come automatically once learnt, for if sheep are going the wrong way you cannot spend time thinking which whistle to use.

Start whistling with the mouth only. Then try the fingers or a plastic whistle. You can, of course, stick to voice only, but in general the human voice does not carry so far or so clearly as a strong, piercing whistle. New Zealand plastic whistles are advertised in some farming papers and *Scottish Sheepdog Handler*, and are not expensive. I find that the plastic whistle has one big advantage. Rain often falls while you are shepherding, and the plastic whistle completely enclosed in your mouth is not affected by wet. If your fingers become wet you may not be able to whistle at all, or the sound may be different to the dog. Remember, if it sounds different, it is different. But do try to avoid the experience of my brother Tot at the end of one triangular drive: the sheep were homeward bound under command, when they suddenly started wandering all over the place and the dog did nothing about it. Later I asked, 'What was the matter with you?' The reply: 'My whistle had blown out of my mouth!'

There are also nose whistles, but they seem big and clumsy to me. Top handlers like Charlie Relph use them, so they must be all right. With all whistles or voice commands it is very important how you give the order. A longer and slower command allows the dog time to think about what's coming, and to adjust its pace accordingly. For example, the 'Stop' whistle is almost universally one long blast. If you give that command in a shorter, sharp fashion, some dogs will collapse their legs under them and skid to a halt from a gallop. In doing so they make grass fly and alarm the sheep quite unnecessarily. Always remember that we are trying to handle stock in the easiest, quietest way possible, and that if they are disturbed needlessly they use extra energy and therefore extra food. Try to give the dog time to absorb the command. Don't upset it by continuous orchestration so that it thinks 'I must always move quickly'. A quick dog, always dashing here and there, does not save time; it makes work.

From this don't get the idea that it doesn't matter whether the dog stops or not. We are talking of fractions of a second. The dog should stop swiftly but gently, and not go into a skid, and the way you give an order helps it to do the right thing. If it is naturally a sharp mover, you must take even more care in the way you give signals.

Sheep can be worked into any given position using only five basic commands. There are others for finer work, but if you and your dog master these five you can carry out most shepherding jobs. The commands are 'Stop', 'Go right', 'Go left' and 'Come on to your sheep'. At the end of the run you want your dog to return to you, for which I say 'Here to me' or 'That'll do'. Others use 'Heel' or 'Come here'. If whistling this command, a single short blast is common.

I have already mentioned the 'Stop' whistle. It is like 'Whoa' to a horse. I believe that a young dog should lie flat when given that long blast. It should go down flat and stay down flat, till told to move. In other chapters I say that too much regimentation is unnecessary, but I do believe in being strict about this with a young dog. If you don't make it lie down flat, it will start to creep about, and by the time the dog is three years old it is tending to do what it wants, and not what you want. I tell this to the trials men, but they don't believe me. Yet this must be so, as our old friend Lennie Greenwood knew when commenting on a suggestion that doubling (running brace) was harmful to a dog's obedience. 'Those that are winning the brace are also winning the singles, because they have taught these dogs to wait,' said Len. Obviously, brace work would become quite impossible if you had no confidence that one dog would stay where you put it while you were working the other.

When working a dog close at hand, quiet signals suffice. The dog becomes accustomed to this mode of working, so when you take it on to a trials field don't alter your policy. Dogs have become thoroughly upset at trials through being treated differently from when at home. Naturally commands must be adjusted as distances increase. It is no use whistling quietly to a dog half a mile away; the command must carry. If using voice only for close work, as is quite permissible, 'Lie down' is better than 'Sit'. Two words are preferable to one, because the dog hears the first part and prepares itself for what is to follow.

My right-hand whistle is 'Whit-whit', two short blasts in quick succession on the same note. I am commanding the dog to go to its own right. Speed and angle can to some extent be controlled by the way the command is given. If the dog is going out and I feel that it will tend to run too tight, I give it a really heavy blast to 'blow' it out. If it is loping too slowly I use a few sharper whistles in quick succession, to encourage it to put on speed. Having learnt the dog's natural speed from past observation, I can help it go faster or slower by the way the commands are given. A dog that swings wider on command while running without change of pace is preferable to one that must be stopped and given a redirection whistle. The former might drop one point in a trial; the latter, two or three.

Voice call for the right hand is 'Away here' or ' 'Way to me'. 'Get out' or 'Get out o' that' are equally suitable but unfashionable. Remember that it does not matter what words are used, provided that they are said in a sufficiently firm tone and that the dog understands them. One last point about the right hand; if the dog has its sheep in front of it on receiving the command, it

53

should come completely round to the front of those sheep if you continue to give it the right hand. This applies equally to the left hand.

My left-hand whistle is one short blast, followed by a long one dropping away, on the same key as the first note: 'Whoa-whoooa'. I like to think that the second part of this whistle is making the dog lift away. As with the right-hand whistle, it is possible to 'blow' the dog out by whistling harder and longer, especially with the second part. My voice command for left hand is 'Come bye'.

If the dog is running too wide, I have a whistle to which all my dogs are trained—'Who-whait', a short note followed by a crisp strike.

The 'Drive' and 'Fetch' whistles are both the same. No matter whether the dog is facing towards you or away from you, you are directing it towards its sheep. We used to have one whistle for 'Drive' and another for 'Fetch' until we found this was unnecessary. My whistle is 'Awee-a'. On receiving this, the dog should walk on towards the centre of its sheep, unless of course it has a very big flock and must work from the sides (*see Chapter* 6). The voice command is 'Walk on'. If the dog is not getting into its work, I give it sharper blasts to quicken it. I don't like such dogs; I prefer one that has to be told to take its time.

This brings us to the 'fringe' commands. 'Stand', as against 'Lie down', 'Steady' or 'Take your time' need no explanation. If I want the dog to come in to a particular spot, as in shedding, 'Come in this' is useful, always accentuating the last syllable, so that the dog has been prepared for it. All these commands should be clear and distinct, spoken with the voice of authority, and not as if next week will do.

One last command: if my dog has gathered its sheep, and I want it to go back for another lot, a new command is needed. I shout 'Look back', followed by the appropriate right- or left-hand whistle when the dog has turned away to try and see the other sheep. Some handlers have a special whistle for this move.

My alternative set of whistles as used for Cap are:

Right hand   Huw-way—two long notes both varying
Left hand   Huy-way Huy-way—short short—long short
Fetch   Hokey-cokey—four of exactly the same length
               going down and up

Stop
Draw in
Look back } Same as right hand, giving dog's name
Heel

6
TRAINING—FIRST STAGES

Sheep dogs can be trained to perform duties which seem to place that animal's intelligence above that of all other animals; and a shepherd without a good dog may be well described as only half a shepherd.

W. J. Malden: *British Sheep and Shepherding*

Serious training does not begin until the pup is over six months old, although with a well grown dog it may occasionally start at four months. The pup's treatment before this is important, however. It should have a kennel with a yard from which it can see comings and goings, but should not be allowed free range. Had the pup been kept shut up all its life, everything would be foreign to it on release for training. Teach the youngster to lead from ten weeks, by all means, and to be tied up, and to 'Lie down' if you have time.

Plate 18 Relaxed concentration from Tot Longton and Ken as the sheep are put out at the famous Longshaw trials, Derbyshire. Hurdles on the left form a Maltese cross, still a popular obstacle through which the sheep are driven before penning.
Plate 19 Tim Longton and Cap in trouble at Longshaw. This sheep broke, and the time whistle sounded before penning was completed.

Plate 20 (top) Roy had better sheep, shown here being turned gradually to face the required direction.

Plate 21 (centre) Going, going . . . Roy stays steady as the sheep are eased into the open pen mouth. The handler must keep hold of the 6 ft rope. Under ISDS rules there is no limit to the length of the crook as exists in New Zealand.

Plate 22 (below) . . . Gone! Roy and Tim Longton achieve a finish which put them in second place. This is the culmination of a trial unless a sheep has to be singled afterwards.

A light chain is best for early leading lessons. If a strap is used the pup may bite through it, and after that it will keep trying to bite through its lead. This is an annoying and energy-wasting habit. Remember that all dogs are different, and that one may walk under leash immediately where another will take several days. The collar must be tight enough to prevent it slipping off, for a dog that gets the habit of slipping its collar is an awful nuisance. When tying the pup up for the first few times, stay with it for a few minutes to give it confidence. You may teach the young dog to lie down by pressing it gently but firmly to the ground, and saying 'Lie down', or whatever your command is to be. It may learn this lesson quickly, but be prepared for it to forget when it starts to run, and you will have to teach it all over again.

The pup should not be introduced to sheep at too young an age. If it finds it cannot keep up with them it may become upset, excited or frightened, and develop bad habits. Far better let it grow until it has plenty of size to outpace the sheep. It must be adequately fed from birth (*see Chapter 2*) for like any other young animal it will never recover from a stunted upbringing. Barking and yapping are other faults which occur when the pup is too small for the sheep, and it may lose its confidence through a knock from an old ewe, especially if she has a lamb with her.

To start training, the ideal is a compact little paddock, certainly not more than two or three acres, with about eight quiet sheep. Naturally you must use whatever field is on hand, but a large acreage is no good. The sheep will be looking for ways of getting to the far end; you may lose your temper; and dog, man and sheep will all be worse rather than better.

Very, very seldom does a dog do things right at the beginning. Anything may happen—or nothing. Working sheep is a natural instinct, and if it isn't there you can't put it there. Although most well bred Border collies begin to run at about six months, they may reach eighteen months before starting and be just as good as the others ultimately. At the beginning the dog's reaction may be simply to chase the sheep, to scatter them in all directions, to bite them or to hold them nicely up to a wall.

To encourage a pup to start work it is a good thing to let it 'have a go'. This is especially so if the dog is easily put off, as so many are today. Let it become 'geared up' so that it wants to carry on. For this very early period it is allowed to do things that would never be tolerated in an older dog. If my advice seems contradictory, I reiterate that I find it easier to check an over-keen dog than to bring on a timid one. Don't worry if it simply flies through the middle in these early stages; another dog may lie down and look at the sheep, but I prefer a pup that starts by being a bit rough; you can smooth off the corners more easily than you can coax an unwilling worker.

One pup that did very well right from the start came from John Richardson at four months old. Bill was sold into Devon on a week's approval. The buyer did nothing with the pup for two or three days, but when he did take it out, it 'froze' on seeing the sheep at the far end of the field. 'I didn't know what to do next, as I had no idea how much training the pup had received,' he told me. 'I gave it a *shhh*ing sound, and Bill set off in a wide arc and gathered all the sheep in the field. I went straight into the house and wrote out my cheque.' Bill went on to win the English National in 1973 for Eric Elliott.

A method recommended by some is to tie the pup to an older dog. This is quite useless. I've tried it, and apart from spoiling the older dog it shows no results. You might think the technique had possibilities in teaching a youngster to run wide where it tended to run tight, but this is not so. Its older partner gets fed up if it has any sense, and I even had one—Ken, I think it was—who set about the trainee because it wouldn't run with him, and would have worried it had I not intervened. Don't waste time with this senseless idea.

Tups should not be used for training pups. They are too strong and rough. They get used to what is happening and come to the handler, where they know they cannot be worked. Try to avoid using the same sheep each time, as they soon refuse to run properly and simply frustrate the pup. Another basic principle is a few minutes every day rather than half an hour once a week.

Never shut up your dog and forget about it for a few days, because it did badly last time. That is all the more reason for taking it out the next day. Never let yourself be exasperated and bad-tempered at the end of a session; be on good terms with the pup when it returns to kennels, no matter how big a mess it has made of its job.

Training a sheep dog is not easy; hours òf training have gone into the apparently effortless co-ordination between man and dog sometimes seen at the top trials, and training to a time-table is out of the question. No dog is born perfect but some begin to work more naturally than others. Because a certain champion was trained in a certain way, that is no reason for following the same method with every pup you possess. Each dog is an individual, and must be treated as such.

Remember the four basic commands 'Stop', 'Go right', 'Go left', 'Come straight on to the sheep'. Away from sheep, the dog may have obeyed the 'Stop' command implicitly, but when it meets a flock it may, in its excitement, forget all it has learnt. Don't worry about this. Such dogs are keen to work, and that is the main thing. The 'Stop' command can be enforced, but don't be too hard, and spoil the youngster's keenness. The way to teach 'Left' and 'Right' is to give the appropriate signal as the dog moves in that direction. In time it will come to associate its action with a certain command, until the day comes when it acts in that way *because of* the command.

When the pup has had its frolic with the sheep in a corner, the next step is to attempt mid-field work. Give the appropriate 'Left' or 'Right' command as the youngster circles the sheep, and try to keep it at a short distance from the flock by moving between it and the sheep. Don't frighten it. As it runs, try to stop it from time to time, using the 'Stop' command. Your biggest problem will be keeping the sheep together, and here an older dog may be of help. Sometimes the presence of an older dog makes the pup keener than ever to bite and jump in, or it may want to chase around with the older dog. There is no hard and fast rule here. Roy would have nothing to do with this helping job when first trained; he used to skulk off home if too much was said, but now he stays indefinitely.

If the pup tries to split the sheep, you must keep it off them. One method is to throw your stick in front of it—don't hit it—and another is to have a pocketful of little stones, though I've not tried that. I think talking helps to quieten a very fast-moving dog, and for this type is preferable to whistling in the early stages. Let the dog fetch the sheep to you, stop it, and call it to heel. Do this time and time again. Change from right hand to left hand, change the angle of setting off, and change the paddock if possible.

At first your trainee will run round the back of you, ie with you between it and the sheep. You must now try to get it to work in front of you, and this is difficult and often tedious. Again, a small field helps. If you begin to feel annoyed, put the dog away with a friendly pat and bring it out again another day. A great deal can be achieved with patience. I have started to train dogs at six months old, and they have been eighteen months before they really got the hang of things. Let the dog think it has done well even if it hasn't, when fastening it up.

A check cord is a useful aid in the early stages for dogs that are too keen and will not stop, or for dogs that will not come close enough to their sheep. A light nylon cord is best. In the case of the dog that will not stop, put it on the cord, set it off, and give the 'Down' command just before it gets to the end of the line. Be ready to hold the cord firmly, and its own momentum ensures that it gets a big jolt if it does not stop. Always give it this 'Down' command before jerking it on the end of the rope, otherwise it will not know what is happening. When you think the lesson has gone home, try without the cord. Sometimes you have won and sometimes you haven't. The dog might think: 'I'm free. I can do what I like again!' I have a pup by Roy that does fairly well on the cord but, when I take it off, he has no intention of either looking at or listening to me. Another by Cap was always wanting to jump in and nip, and if I scolded too much he didn't want to run at all. Only at eighteen months old is he getting the message.

Your youngster may not like working near its sheep. Put on the cord, use quiet sheep, and stand on the opposite side of them to the dog, with the cord over or under the sheep. Ask it to walk up, and draw it by the cord if it is reticent. This is the only way I know to bring a dog up to its sheep. I much prefer the dog that has to be kept back, however. You can get between it and the sheep to keep it back, but you can't run round the outside and drive it in.

The way to make a dog stop is to work on it continually. Whistle it down, send it on a yard or two, then blow it down again. My young Ben is now ten months, and he doesn't like stopping. I give him the 'Stop' signal, and if he doesn't stop I scold him. Shep is another who doesn't like stopping—or didn't. Now a year and a week old, he is whistled 'Down' almost as soon as he has set off on a fresh command, and he has come to accept it. When I say 'Down' to a young dog, I mean 'Down', and not crouching or edging forward. In training, start the youngster off from well behind you, placing yourself between it and the sheep. Give the right- or left-hand command to set it off, and stop it as it is level with you. You are then positioned to act in case of disobedience. Be consistent at all times; do not be severe to the dog one evening and let it indulge in slipshod behaviour the next.

This applies equally to work. Practical tasks are the best training of all, but when you start to take the youngster with you you must be able to correct its faults. Nothing matures a dog like work, and it is balderdash to say that trials dogs should not work. If a dog runs better on the right than on the left hand, you must persevere with the left, and run it far more on that side than on the other. This all takes time.

On chastisement, let the punishment fit the crime—and the dog. Some dogs have to be threatened or possibly touched with the stick, whereas others would leave you given the same treatment. Dogs are bred with so fine a temperament nowadays that they are soon upset. Pulling a dog's ears a bit is generally the limit of physical punishment.

7

TRAINING—LATER STAGES

In driving a number of sheep to any distance, a well-trained dog never fails to confine the sheep to the road; he watches every avenue that leads from it, where he takes his stand, threatening every delinquent; and pursues the stragglers, forcing them into the ranks without doing them any injury.

Loudon's *Encyclopaedia of Agriculture* (1883)

We have reached the stage where the dog can gather its few sheep in a little field and bring them to you or hold them against a wall. It will stop—more or less—on command, and return to heel. It has some idea of right and left. The next stage is to move into a rather larger field, still with quiet sheep. The dog's main shortcomings are to be improved. If it is a tight runner, whistle the sheep into a bunch and position yourself between them and the dog, having made it lie down, then give the 'Right' or 'Left' command. You can run alongside it to keep it out, or give the appropriate 'Right' or 'Left' to encourage a new direction, or use your stick, but don't hit the dog. It must become accustomed to the stick and have faith in it. If you have no faith in yourself, leave your stick at home.

If the dog tends to pull up on its outrun, give it a whistle or shoo it along. If it is a wide runner, set it off from near your feet, and direct it initially at a narrower angle to the sheep. I don't believe in teaching a dog to follow the field boundary regardless of where the sheep are. The dog's job is to save time working stock, not to waste it. A dog that invariably follows the wall or hedge is not in contact with its sheep if they are grazing nearer the centre. When first gathering in a bigger field, your pup may gather the first few sheep and leave the rest. This is to be expected; try again.

Some dogs seem 'drawn' by the sheep they have gathered. They approach them too closely. You must be there to teach them to keep their distance when they are behind the sheep and have them in a fairly compact bunch. Use tact here. Don't knock all confidence out of the dog.

The next stage is to get the dog to bring the sheep towards you. Again quiet sheep are a great asset. The dog must learn to come on to its sheep; whether you are in front of it or behind should be immaterial from the dog's point of view. I am now speaking of the small flock of eight or twelve; large numbers call for a different technique, as they must be continually pressed in from either side, or they wander all over the place. Should your dog tend to wander from side to side, stop it, and bring it straight on. The Border collie that comes straight on to its sheep is better than a 'weaving' dog. Some dogs are natural weavers, and one object of training is to discourage this habit. Try to get the sheep to run away from the dog, fetch it on, and stop it whenever it tries to move sideways. If a dog is for trials work and gets this weaving habit, it will never have a good 'Fetch' or 'Drive', because the sheep will never be in a straight line.

To bring the dog on to its sheep, use the appropriate command discussed in Chapter 5. Remember that while the dog's natural instinct is to gather sheep and bring them to the handler, driving sheep away from the handler is quite foreign to the dog's inherent instinct and previous experience and training. Some learn easily, others take a long, long time. Walk by your little flock of quiet sheep with the dog by your side. Then push the sheep's heads away, call in your dog, and try to get it to follow behind. If it wanders too far to the left, give it the 'Right' whistle, and vice versa. You can't really force the pace when teaching driving. Patience, perseverance and still more patience are needed.

I had a grand little dog called Joe, who couldn't get the message at all. We tried driving for week after week, with no results at all, then one evening everything snapped into place. Joe suddenly realised, 'Oh, you want me to go behind them,' and he would have taken those sheep half a mile there and then. He never looked back, and was placed in trials at just over one year. A great little dog was Joe; he delighted his new owner when I sold him.

A narrow lane is quite useful for teaching the drive. If filled with sheep, there is no side for the dog to pass, so it must stay behind. Some men have put up double fencing for the purpose. Keep up the 'Right' and 'Left' commands, and the dog will soon find that the sheep are leaving it, and that that is what the handler wants. Again, ten minutes once or preferably twice a day is better than a long session every few days.

A dog that daren't run past sheep in a lane is as bad as one that won't drive. If you pass your gate with the sheep still trotting along, it's an awful long time before you get to their heads if the dog daren't pass them. All dogs are not good road dogs, while others excel, and slip along to guard familiar gaps.

Never allow former lessons to be forgotten while teaching the drive. The next stage is cutting the sheep in two; shedding or singling. To single means taking one sheep only, and is difficult; never teach this first. To develop the shed, return to your quiet bunch of sheep, standing on one side with your dog on the other. String the sheep out with your hands, and as soon as there is a suitable gap, ask your dog to come right through to you. This

66

practice may do the most good of anything we have yet attempted, especially if the sheep fight a bit, and the dog discovers it can boss them.

You may step towards the dog, but it must come right through to you, and the way it comes is vital. It must come quickly, without snapping at the sheep. A positive, sharp movement on the dog's part splits the sheep and sends them nicely apart. If your dog doesn't come through far enough or quickly enough, the sheep will simply go round you and re-unite. Obviously that is the opposite of what is intended.

Don't spend a whole session on teaching the shed. Let it be just a few minutes during or at the end of the practice. The dog should be taught that one lot of the sheep is to be driven away, and to turn those sheep to help their departure. Encourage with a snap of the fingers and praise when the youngster tries to do well. Then help it to keep the shed sheep away; don't bother about holding the others in these early stages.

Not all dogs are born shedders, but if a dog likes the job it may shed or single when it shouldn't. At an Alston, Cumbria, trial in my very early days, someone suggested teaching the single first, but my father said: 'Don't practise singling too much, or your dog may single when it ought to be penning.' After the collie is competent at shedding a few sheep, gradually reduce numbers till it is shedding just one—the single. To take a single correctly, open the sheep so that there is room between the last one and the rest. The dog should come through to the head of the sheep. Don't overdo this. If the dog doesn't like singling it will get sick of its training; if it enjoys the move it may do too much and single at every opportunity.

A strong-eyed dog makes shedding or singling difficult. The sheep flock together for mutual protection. The 'eye' denotes concentration. We want just enough to give the right amount of concentration. Alan Jones' Roy has very, very little eye, but its relaxed manner without letting the sheep go has won a lot of trials. A dog with a lot of eye is holding itself very tight, and this is transmitted to the sheep, which are in a tremor—exactly what

67

you do not want for easy working. The first impression made by the dog on the sheep is vital, and sheep approached by a strong-eyed dog are more likely to freeze up. Though a dog with little eye may not look as stylish, its easy concentration enables it to be on the best terms with its sheep. Dogs without eye can hold their sheep equally well. The character was bred in from setters— shooting dogs selected to remain steady. In the Border collie world, a dog that 'sticks' is a terrible time waster. Fortunately they are less common now, but a few people still have to shout their heads off to raise their dogs.

No dog is competent unless it will leave the sheep it is working, and go back for another lot on command. This is a new step for the dog, and calls for much patience. Until now we have brought out the trainee's inherent concentration, ensuring that it keeps its mind on its job and thinks about nothing in the world except those sheep that it is actually working. Now we must teach it to leave them, however nicely they are under control, and seek some more sheep that (on hill ground) may be out of sight altogether. This is an occasion when we must really put ourselves in the dog's place, and realise that things that are perfectly obvious to us are beyond the dog's knowledge at that moment. We know that there are some more sheep over the hump of the hill, and that we need them home with the rest; the dog doesn't.

The first stage, therefore, is to teach the dog to look away from the sheep it is working, on command. Do this while shedding. Your dog has come nicely between the sheep and split one lot away, as it has been taught so often. It works these that it has held, while the others wander off. The latter have been no concern of your youngster in the past, so you must now make it understand that a new development is under way. As it works its group, go between the dog and the sheep and make it look round. As it does so, give it the 'blow-back' whistle if you plan to use one, followed immediately by the 'Left' or 'Right' according to which way it is to take these other sheep.

The sheep you have shed off must be allowed to wander a little distance away before you give your 'Look back' command; but

68

not too far, otherwise the dog will not see them closely enough to make it realise that they are now its concern. Remember all the time that you are teaching your dog to do the direct opposite of all its previous lessons, so be patient. Don't carry on the exercise many times in succession, or the pupil will start looking back when it should be doing something else.

In effect, you are making the dog change its mind, so that it knows that it has to work to *your* mind. As it learns to turn round when you ask it, don't let it go back to the same side every time. If it prefers the right hand, emphasise practice on the left hand, a principle that applies throughout training. The most difficult part is to get your dog to turn round on command in the first place; once you have relaxed its concentration on those sheep it is working, and directed its thoughts to another lot, you are on the way to success.

This 'going back' business warrants far more attention than most people give it. The dog must not only 'go back', it must go back in a specified direction. People often say: 'My dog will go back!', and so it does, anywhere it likes. When sent back, many a dog thinks: 'I'm off!' and the handler can't stop it. If your dog develops this trait, stop it before it has run very far. Then set it off again, and keep on doing so until it is under command whatever the distance.

I prefer voice commands for the 'Go back'. A good pair of lungs are every bit as effective as a special whistle, whether close at hand or working at a distance. In my first International at Blackpool, I shouted to Nell: 'Away back out of that!', and I've never had a better go-back.

When your dog is going back competently to retrieve sheep it has just shed at close quarters, go into a bigger field. Gather some sheep to the centre, but make sure others are left at one end. Never, now or any time, deliberately send your dog to places where you know there are no sheep. Nothing causes more lack of confidence in you. Of course, there are times on the hill when a shepherd must send a dog back to check that there is nothing left, but a mature dog understands this. If you sent it twice to the same place for no sheep, it would be upset, and quite rightly. At the *Daily Express* Hyde Park trials, I was asked to run Ken and Cap without any sheep, just to demonstrate their reactions to direction whistles. I wasn't too keen, but *Daily Express* did such a wonderful job for the Border collie world that I could not refuse. Ken was six then, Cap only two. Both ran splendidly the first time, but Cap refused to believe there were no sheep, and set off again to look for them. He would have gone into the Serpentine if I'd asked. Ken, on the other hand, was a mature, fully experienced dog. After his first vain run he returned, and set off again with marked reluctance to my command. When he came back, implicit in his look was: 'You may be mad, but I'm not. I've been down twice and there is nothing. I'm not here to be made a fool of and I'm not going any more.' Nor did he; he stood at my feet and refused to run, whatever I said. This is a classic example of the difference between a young and a mature dog.

Teaching a dog to go back is not as hard as teaching to drive; when a dog gains faith in you, it likes to go back. When you move to a bigger field, and have your dog with sheep in the centre, its position before setting off for those you have left at the far end is vital. Position the dog between the sheep it has in the centre and those it must now fetch. Stop it. Stand opposite to it, across the centre of the flock. If you have sheep in the top right-hand corner, and you wish the dog to gather them right-handed, move some paces to your left. Give the collie some left hand, so that it is still opposite you. Signal the 'Go back' so that it looks round. Setting off from this position, your dog should now swing away right-handed, and come up behind its second lot of sheep correctly. By starting from the correct position you leave it with less ground in which to set off on the wrong side and so misdirect the sheep.

Instil such obedience that the dog 'claps' or lies flat whenever it gets the 'Stop' whistle, and continue this at ever greater distances. At all times remember previous lessons, because some dogs will move on a stage yet completely forget what they have been taught previously. Your youngster may be trying its hardest to get the message in this 'Go back' business, so don't get out of temper with failure. Handlers who whistle a great deal are no help to a dog trying to learn its job. If it is not under command when going back, it might as well not set off, for it may miss the sheep altogether in broken ground if it doesn't go back on the course you require. Dogs react differently when they are a long way from their handler. I had one that, if sent round the outside of the fell to gather, clung to the wall and at no time came in to its sheep. It was quite useless for fell work, because it would circle the ground completely yet not stir a single sheep. I sold it to an in-bye farmer on flat marshland, with every sheep in sight, and he thought it was a great dog.

No two dogs are the same. Some are ideal for gathering a large number of sheep, yet too keen with a few. I had a dog called Ben; at two and a half years old he was a big, rampaging sort of dog that dashed round the fell wall, but when he had the sheep gathered he brought them along as steadily as could be. Put him with a small packet, as in a trial, and he was far too keen. Dogs must learn to conserve their energies, and they find this with growing experience. I had a newly broken dog that had been helping to gather 500 sheep from a big hill. As we went down with the flock, this hot-headed dog was so exhausted that she could scarcely put one leg in front of the other. She was so tired that she could not possibly have got into any mischief even if she had been so inclined, so I left her, and eventually she staggered into the yard. She took care not to get into such a condition again.

The culminating act of sheep work is penning. Your collie may have gathered the sheep from a scattered hill to perfection, fetched them to you and driven them home in front of you. It may have shed off those you didn't want, but until the sheep are in the folds there is no question of starting mass flock treatment. Penning is therefore vital. It is a test of man's and dog's ability to read sheep. Very rarely does rushing about do any good. 'If you want to win trials, don't get in a hurry,' advised my father forty years ago, and the same applies today and to all sheep work.

In a trial, the unfortunate handler has to pen sheep into a small opening without any supporting barrier. At work, the sheep must be pushed through a gate flanked by a wall or a fence, but of course considerably more animals are likely to be involved. When a big lot of sheep are to be penned, forget about your 'classy' dog. One with power is needed, but not a dog that runs in and tears at the sheep. In New Zealand special dogs are kept for special purposes, but I like to think that mine are all-rounders. Biting is a very bad fault, as in a crowded yard disease germs are easily picked up. A free-working dog is preferable to one with a lot of eye, that stands or lies in one place. The idea is just sufficient eye to retain concentration on the job.

If a dog is weak, daren't face the sheep, or shows any give-back whatsoever, the sheep will know immediately. They spot weakness in a dog when you have noticed nothing. In fact, the first sign will be that the sheep are pushing the dog out. Some dogs bark, but this trait is unfashionable in Britain. It has its uses, however, though more in rocky situations than when penning. Lakeland Herdwicks are unique among British sheep in that they will lie low in cover and let the dogs pass them by. When I was patrol shepherd in Mardale I knew there were some Herdwicks on a fellside, but I couldn't see them till they moved. Barking dogs are an advantage here.

Penning is simply an extension of other work. When sheep have been worked in a proper manner they accept the dog's discipline, and they are penned far more readily than badly shepherded stock. Dogs should be taught to pen as soon as they can do simple tasks, and nothing educates a dog like work. Never forget this, and don't make the common mistake of wearing out the old dogs and ignoring the youngsters. A sheep dog's working life is comparatively short, and you need replacements at hand. Give them a chance. Bring the young dog into routine work at every opportunity, even if it takes a few minutes longer than sticking to the old. The way some men handle dogs is pitiful. 'If a sheep stamps its foot at the dog, it turns tail,' complained one farmer. Yet he would spend £200 or £300 on a good tup, while buying poorly-bred pups and then neglecting them. I can go up a field with Roy on one side and Cap on the other, doing any job among sheep as it comes up. That is as it should be, and that is the whole purpose of this book.

In all aspects of Border collie training, do remember that there is a vast difference between dogs. This has intensified in recent years, and while some are temperamentally as hard as nails, others are extremely soft and 'touchy'. To show what I mean, I will outline training methods on two entirely different Border collies, Ben and Roy. Ben was strong as a horse, in the sense of being strong-willed. Roy was, and is, very sensitive.

Ben came to me as a pup. He had to accept a lot more discipline than Roy, who was a year old when I bought him, though that is not the point. Roy didn't need discipline so much; he was always anxious to please. The main thing was not to upset him. Ben on the other hand was so hard and keen that it was extremely difficult to make him stop. He appeared to be swearing under his breath when I admonished him, and had no intention of taking any notice whatsoever if he had any option. This was particularly marked when teaching him 'Stop' when on his 'Right' and 'Left'. When I brought him round the sheep, he didn't want to stop until he had got in front of them, so anxious was he that they might escape altogether. My cure was to give the 'Stop' command as soon as Ben moved. He was so keen that I had to give the 'Down' command almost before he started; he was half a move in front of me unless I watched what I was doing the whole time.

Ben had no trouble learning the actual 'Right' and 'Left' directions. He was always pressing at his sheep, which in my opinion is a very good point in a young dog. A good outrunner, he soon learnt to drive. It was just this unwillingness to stop once he had reached a certain position round his sheep and away from me. The man who eventually bought him saw him twelve months previously at a year old, and thought he was too desperate a character altogether. Now that he has calmed down, his new owner thinks the world of him.

Roy's owner specially wanted me to have him. He had done a bit of work, all he needed was confidence. It would have been so easy to have shaken his confidence altogether, and the same applies today at seven years old. If all was going well, Roy was all right; but if things went awry, he lacked confidence to go in and put them right. In his first winter of nursery trials he let me down several times, solely from this cause. He would take his sheep three-quarters of the way round the course in fine style, and then suddenly become uncertain. I had to coax and coax him to carry on as he had been doing; any loss of temper or threats would have been disastrous. Yet he has become a national champion.

He had only been here a month when I took him with me round the lambing fields. We came across a ewe whose only lamb had drowned in a small lake. I took the van to transport the ewe home, but Roy wouldn't help me catch it. He wouldn't even look at it, and I had to drive home, not in the best of humours, to fetch another dog. At that stage Roy hadn't the confidence to tackle a single sheep. It was probably something new in his experience, particularly as the ewe was wild and running about a bit, having lost its lamb. He took quite a time to gain confidence to come through to single. Now he is as good a singling dog as I've had.

At invitation trials at Glasgow in June 1975, over a National course, I had penned with Roy, and was stringing the sheep out for the single. Roy saw a gap, 'I know what happens here' was his attitude, and he was through before I asked him, so completing his run.

It's not how they start that matters, it's how they finish.

Plate 23 Classes for fittest or best-looking collie are held in conjunction with trials. The majority of ISDS members are against show standards for Border collies governed by any other body.

Plate 24 Dogs are examined for progressive retinal atrophy, a hereditary disease which has been brought under control by barring registrations of offspring from affected dogs under ISDS rules.

Plate 25 Shepherds' art: collection of crooks at York. Birds and dogs have been incorporated in a craft that now has wide appeal outside sheep farming's ranks.
Plate 26 A happy group of triallists after the English National event at Ambleside, Lake District. There was much rain, but wet weather does not halt trials any more than it does practical shepherding.

8

TRIALS—OUTRUN, FETCH AND DRIVE

*There is no good flock without a good shepherd, and no good
shepherd without a good dog.*

French Shepherds' Club motto,
adopted by ISDS

A sheep dog trial is the ultimate test of intensive training. It is
quite useless to think of trialling unless your dog is completely
under your command. If a man really wants to learn about dogs
and sheep, he should enter a trial. He will then see how easy it
looks and how hard it is. A very little error suffices to put him
out of the reckoning, for at home a mistake by the man or the
dog probably covers itself up shortly afterwards. On the trials
field the same error means that the judge has deducted a point
and cannot put it back.

Given a dog under proper command, the next essential is
temperament. A shy and nervous dog probably won't do as well
in public, though it may be a perfectly acceptable worker at
home. Dogs behave differently at trials compared with familiar

surroundings, and you can never be really sure until you have tried.

By all means set up a trials course at home, though this is for the handler's benefit rather than the dog's. Beginners can gain course experience, especially on the drive, in judging the sheep's distance from the hurdles. Practice penning may also help; I never do this now, though I sometimes wish I had.

If you know no one in the local sheep dog world yet wish to attend a trial, the International Sheep Dog Society secretary can be contacted. If his staff have not been informed of every single trial, they will certainly be able to put you in touch with a local handler.

During the winter, nursery trials are held in many sheep areas. These have gained in popularity in recent years, and have the great advantage of cheapness. No £1 entry fees here; 20p is usual. Another asset is that the director will let you complete your run however badly you have fared, whereas at an Open trial you may be signalled off before you or your dog has had that much-needed practice.

On arrival, give your name to the course director or secretary. Nursery trials are informal affairs, and you are assured a friendly welcome. There will also be a few dozen expert pairs of eyes considering what your dog would do in their hands! Watch several dogs run before taking the field yourself. Observe the sheep; are they quiet, biddable, wild, even or erratic? Decide whether you prefer to run the course right- or left-handed, bearing in mind that the action of the sheep on release may cause you to change your mind. If the lie of the land allows it, contrive to drive your sheep into the hill rather than down it, because they run so much faster downhill that command is difficult.

Try not to fall to the temptation of taking an immature dog to a trial before it is really ready. This trait is increasing, and I don't like it. How many of these youngsters ever reach an Open trial?

A few minutes before you are due to run, exercise your dog, so that it opens its bowels and does not stop to do so when under way. A drink should be unnecessary beforehand, unless the journey has been very hot and long, but don't forget to offer a drink after the run. Try and keep a relaxed attitude, for if you are tense this will be communicated immediately to the dog and thence to the sheep, so increasing your difficulties.

Your name has been called. The moment has arrived. Do not hurry. The stop-watch is not yet ticking. Take out your dog calmly, and from such a point that your starting post is directly in line with the sheep. This is a big help to the dog, indicating in which direction it must seek its sheep. You should be able to see the sheep, the pen men, or both. A dog of trials standard will let you know when it has seen the sheep, by that characteristic jerk of concentration—pulling itself together. Yet if a dog won't look for its sheep, you can't make it. My brother Tot's old Lad never would look at his sheep; he simply stood there with his head down, and if Tot tried to coax him to look, Lad edged closer and closer and put his head further and further down as though he was going to bury himself. The funny thing was that Lad always set off right; he never made a mistake. Perhaps he had seen his sheep as he entered the field. Other dogs scan the field, and tense themselves on seeing the sheep. When Roy has done this, he *always* gives me a glance which seems to say, 'When you're ready, I am.'

This prior positioning is vitally important. If the dog doesn't set off right, it can't finish right. Scottish shepherd Peter Hetherington is an artist at placing a dog before it runs. It is quite a performance when he sets Nell off, turning her bodily to the desired angle, and Nell was good enough to win the Shepherds' Championship at the 1973 Bala centenary trials, where she also gained the Lord Mostyn championship cup and the J. S. Gray trophy for the Scottish dog or bitch scoring highest points in National and International trials.

Your dog's setting-off position should be within a few yards of you. If further away, it might appear to the judges to be out of command, or seeking unfair advantage. There is a post at the top of the field which is the sheep's position, and don't set off until they are near it, and quiet. If the sheep are going pell-mell some-

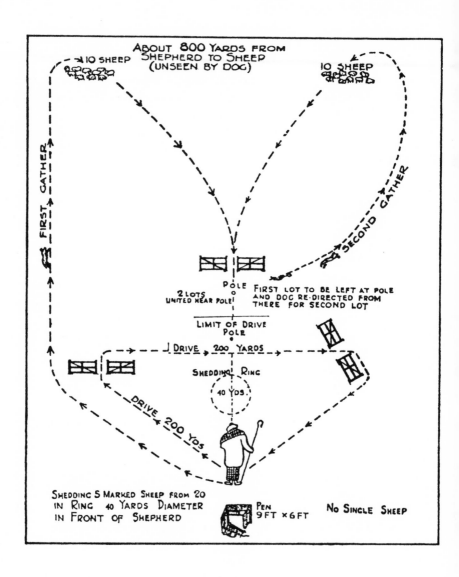

ABOUT 800 YARDS FROM
SHEPHERD TO SHEEP
(UNSEEN BY DOG)

10 SHEEP

10 SHEEP

FIRST GATHER

SECOND GATHER

POLE

2 LOTS
UNITED NEAR POLE

FIRST LOT TO BE LEFT AT POLE
AND DOG RE-DIRECTED FROM
THERE FOR SECOND LOT

LIMIT OF DRIVE
POLE

DRIVE 200 YARDS

SHEDDING RING

40 YDS.

DRIVE 200 YDS

SHEDDING 5 MARKED SHEEP FROM 20
IN RING 40 YARDS DIAMETER
IN FRONT OF SHEPHERD

PEN
9 FT × 6 FT

NO SINGLE SHEEP

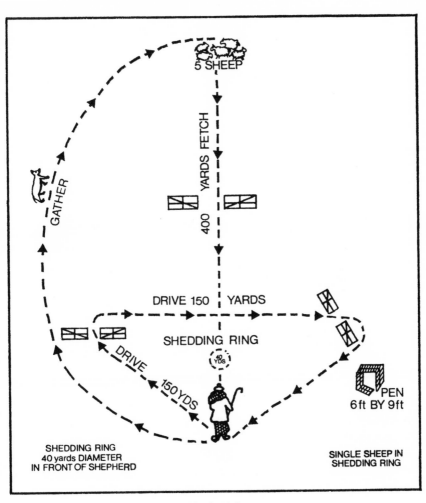

5 SHEEP

GATHER

400 YARDS FETCH

DRIVE 150 YARDS

SHEDDING RING

40 YDS

DRIVE

150 YDS

PEN
6ft BY 9ft

SHEDDING RING
40 yards DIAMETER
IN FRONT OF SHEPHERD

SINGLE SHEEP IN
SHEDDING RING

Two typical trial courses

where, don't set off at all—unless the course director says you must. At some trials no attempt is made to place the sheep; they are just let out of a creep hole. Your practical experience of your dog is vital at the start. If it tends to run tight, stand it so that it has to turn its head to see the sheep, speak to it and set it squarer. Be ready to switch the dog to the other hand if the sheep move away from what is practical for your intended direction of gather. A wide runner should be brought up to you, then set off straighter.

Not until you are satisfied that you have done all to prepare your dog should you give the word 'Go'. This is either a spoken command or one of your direction whistles, 'Right' or 'Left' according to which side you are running the dog. I reiterate that the timekeeper's watch does not start until the dog leaves its handler. If the dog is a fast runner, give it a quiet vocal command, possibly just *'shhh'*. If sluggish, a sharp whistle is more likely to quicken it. You are now on trial as well as the dog, so try and give these initial commands so that they will last as long as possible; redirection, quickening or steadying signals will from now on lose points. At an English National at Windermere I gave Snip the slightest 'click-click' of my tongue immediately after she had started. I thought none but she would hear it, but Bob Fraser and Llyr Evans in the judges' box behind me heard, and docked me half a point each. I lost that championship by half a point.

The ideal outrun is pear-shaped, with the handler standing at the stalk of the pear. As the dog passes the sheep to gather, it is as far away from them as at any time, and only when it is well behind them should it turn towards them. To achieve perfection, the dog must follow this course of its own accord, without any prompting or redirecting. On a small trials field such a feat is quite possible; on International fields with a half-mile outrun, extra commands are usually needed.

I don't favour a Border collie that goes like a bullet. Neither should it dawdle; the pace should be just as fast as it can keep up all day. You are sending it for specific sheep in a specific place.

Though redirection commands will lose you points, the loss would be far greater if the dog carried on unchecked in the wrong direction, so be ready to use commands. A slow runner may be sharpened up with a '*shoo*' or a whistle, a dog going too straight 'blown out' by the appropriate 'Right' or 'Left', and a wide runner brought in similarly, though this is seldom necessary.

The dog is now passing its sheep, whether unaided or after redirections. It has the sheep in its eye as it turns in towards them. You, the handler, are a long way off, but you want it to come in at a sensible distance behind them. There is no fixed guide here; it depends on the dog, the sheep and the field. In some cases fifty yards is a good distance, but on a small field there is not fifty yards to play with. A strong dog commands sheep at a far greater distance than a weak one, and some sheep will stand a dog close to them when others turn tail and gallop. Thus your dog must be far enough away at the furthest point of its outrun not to upset the sheep; if it is too far away it takes longer to come on to its sheep, which is not practical shepherding. The outrun ends at this point where the dog stops, or should stop. To be correct, the sheep should be aware of the dog when it pulls up. There is no law which states that the dog must actually stop, but it is better if it pulls up momentarily, giving the sheep a chance to see it, and then sets off kindly but straight towards them. This first impression makes a tremendous difference to your run.

If the sheep are at their stake, the point where the dog should pull up is usually at 12 o'clock, assuming that the sheep are at the clock centre and the handler at 6 o'clock. Sometimes, however, a dog will pull up at 1 o'clock on a right-hand run, because it has seen something that you have not. Some slight movement of the sheep communicates itself to the dog, or it may even be instinctive anticipation. All that matters is whether the sheep move directly from where they are towards the first obstacle. If they do, the dog's positioning cannot be wrong. There is a point of balance that neither judge nor handler can always see.

I prefer a dog that goes round to 11 o'clock on a right-hand

83

run, to one that habitually stops at 1 o'clock. It is easier to stop the dog that is passing its sheep than to encourage a dog that has not quite reached the desired target.

During the lift, dogs should neither flop from side to side nor be continually getting up and lying down. If the former, it is a sign that the dog lacks power to lift the sheep, and in the latter case it probably has too much eye. If the dog lifts the sheep correctly, they move towards the first obstacle sited half-way down the fetch part of the course, see p 98.

A brisk walk is the best pace for the fetch. Don't be thinking about speed at this stage; you will not run out of time through taking the fetch at a sensible pace. The ideal dog keeps well behind during the fetch, not so close to its sheep that they go faster all the time, nor yet so far off that they start grazing. A dog that works 'heavy' sheep correctly needs to be further back when working wild sheep.

In Ireland in October 1974 Jim Cropper and I represented England. Jim ran Clyde, who gathered well, but the sheep set off down the field like rockets. Clyde had to flank them to hit the first obstacle, which they did, but then Jim stopped his dog until the sheep were half way to the handler's stake. Jim knew enough about sheep and dogs to take the risk that the flock would come straight towards him although the dog had lost contact with them, which they did, and the pair won that International-style trial. This shows very clearly that, though you can only do what the sheep will let you, some men handle sheep better than others. Experience of both sheep and dogs counts a lot. If sheep are fickle, you must have your dog lying well off them, yet in a position to move when necessary. On the fetch the dog should not go from side to side all the time, or the sheep will corkscrew and points will be lost.

During this time the handler stays at his post, or within a yard or two. If he moves further away, the judges may deduct points. The turn at the end of the fetch should be behind the stake, as tight to it as possible. The ideal is for the sheep to have their heads straight for the next obstacle as they come out of the turn.

If the dog is not brought round soon enough, they may wander to the left on a left-handed course; if it comes round too quickly, they may set off too fast. It is essential to watch both sheep and dog on the turns. If a bad start is made after turning the corner, the dog will have to flank from side to side, upsetting the sheep. See that it doesn't tighten on to its sheep too much just as they turn.

As the sheep reach the handler and turn the corner, the fetch ends and the drive begins. This calls for the same commands as the fetch, for the dog is still driving the sheep away from it. After the turn, let the dog slowly drift in behind its sheep, and try to keep them in line for the next hurdle. You will already have ascertained whether the hurdle is a 'drive' or a 'pull-through' which the sheep have to go round and then turn back through. Above all, try and keep the pace steady.

The handler's major difficulty arrives at the next hurdle, ie the first obstacle on the drive. If kept straight, the sheep should drift through the middle of a 'drive' hurdle, but you must have your dog in a handy position to turn them. It must not be too far behind, yet on the other hand the sheep may go too fast if it comes too near them. Experience and anticipation are what count here; judging the sheep's position relative to the hurdle is by no means easy. If the sheep go faster than you would like, the dog must still be kept within range of them, or it will never be in time to turn them at the next obstacle. I remember running Ken in the Farmers' Championship at Alnwick, Northumberland, on some very fickle Scottish Blackface hoggs. I can see those sheep going yet with their tails swinging over their backs. Ken had to be kept going or he would have been out of range altogether. They were going dead straight for the obstacles; just before they reached it I set Ken off to turn them, which he did successfully. After that they settled down.

Does a dog know that the sheep should go through the hurdles? I believe that some do. 'White' Harry Huddleston, running his old Kep, tried to make him come to the side as the hurdle was approached. Harry argued with his old dog over the distance of the course, but Kep, usually biddable, took no notice, and the sheep went through correctly. If he had responded to the whistles he would have sent his sheep wrong, and Harry is adamant that the dog knew what should happen. On another occasion running young Nell, I misjudged the first hurdle, bringing the sheep round sharp on my side of the near hurdle. When they reached the next obstacle after the cross drive, Nell nipped in unbidden and shaved them past the hurdle, again on the wrong side. It seemed to me that Nell was saying: 'It's all right boss. I've got the idea. Just leave things to me.' If I hadn't made a mistake initially, it would have been fine.

These incidents demonstrate how difficult it is to judge obstacles at a distance on the triangular drive, even after much experience. This is especially so if the field is flat and the grass mown short. On approaching the first hurdle on the drive, it is sometimes a good policy to direct your dog momentarily to the side, to give better idea of the distance between it and the hurdle, but this is getting rather advanced. You must immediately re-direct your dog to its original position, or the sheep will be moved out of line.

Like so many moves, you can only do this if the sheep will let you. It's a grand thing when they are 'heavy', allowing a dog to work close to them. Then it can whip past at the last second and turn them through the hurdle. Once the sheep are through, see that the dog does not go through right on their tails, or they may set off at full gallop. Far better if the dog slips round the far hurdle, well away from them.

Skill in turning this corner governs what sort of a cross-drive you will have. Try to stop the dog at the right point so that the sheep head directly for the last obstacle. This section of the course is called the cross-drive, and should be in a straight line. That does not entail the dog keeping straight; it may have to flank on one side continually to maintain the requisite direction. The object is to keep the sheep straight, not the dog. Nor is it necessarily a good drive because both hurdles are cleared. Passing through the hurdles yet corkscrewing about in between may lose more points than a straight drive culminating in last-second miss at the hurdles. When John Richardson won the Supreme with Wiston Cap in 1965, he missed the last obstacle with every sheep, yet otherwise he had a tremendous run.

A pull-through obstacle is rather more difficult than a drive-through. The dog must be positioned ready to turn the sheep into the former, whereas with the latter they are turned after safely clearing the hurdle. When the third and last obstacle has been cleared, one third of the triangular drive remains—the home run. Remember, this is still part of the trial, and the sheep must be kept to as straight a line as possible as they return to the handler. Don't become casual, or allow them to drift. Some dogs are better drive dogs than others, and will keep the sheep to their job with less prompting. Wait at your post until the sheep enter the shedding ring; after that you may go to meet them.

9

TRIALS—SHED, PEN AND SINGLE

*Hill land would be valueless but for the dogs. It is too high
and bleak to carry any stock but sheep, and without dogs the
sheep would be uncontrollable. I do not suppose a couple of
hundred men could gather Dyffryn mountain unaided.
Thirteen men can manage with dogs.*

Thomas Firbank: *I Bought A Mountain* (1940)

We will assume that the next move is shedding, as it is in the
National and the International. In the National, two sheep are
ribboned and three unmarked. Your task is to shed off two unmarked sheep. To do this, put your dog to the other side of the
flock, and try and work the two sheep needed to one end or the
other. It looks more spectacular if three leave and the dog comes
to the head of those two to be shed. A shed will not be deemed
completed if the sheep still face one another; if the shed sheep
turn round, that should do. A good shedding dog will nip
through quickly, and by its very action turn the sheep's heads
away. Yet it is not always either possible or advisable to try to
head the sheep to be shed; each situation varies.

To shed the two sheep required is more difficult than it sounds, although you have one to play with. One big point about shedding—the sooner it is done, the easier it is. When the sheep have been turned several times, and the dog has tried or half-tried to come through between them, they get to know what is happening, and cluster together with their heads down. Alan Jones was once in all sorts of trouble at the shed. His sheep had bunched, just as described. Alan ran his stick along the ground, then 'whooshed' with his arms, and the sheep strung out. Fortunately, the two he wanted were at one end, so he called his dog through and completed the shed. A lot of men would have made a mess of this move.

Another move that none but a thoroughly experienced professional sheep man could accomplish was Jim Wilson's shed at the Edinburgh International. Jim had sheep all round him in ones and twos, instead of shedding into just two groups as is customary. Having retained his necessary five and shed off fifteen, he had the problem of bringing his five through the rest to the pen to prove wrong all those who thought it couldn't be done.

E. L. Daniel and Harry Huddleston had outstanding sheds at the Towyn International in 1968. Here is the description from *The Field*:

One of the fascinations of Trials are their uncertainty. On this occasion the Welsh Mountain sheep were very even and reasonably tractable, and weather conditions did not vary much throughout. Nonetheless, there is an element of luck in the shedding ring especially, and those who know that consistent Lancastrian Harry Huddleston, with Laddie, shared his delight in the way sheep after sheep peeled away from the others, leaving, in a matter of seconds, the five red-collared ewes just as required! Despite this, the pair had to be content with seventh place.

Runner up in the Supreme Championship was E. L. Daniel with Chip. His shed was even more remarkable. Chip cut off five unwanted ewes from the bunch of twenty. They stayed inside the forty yards ring, under the power of Chip's eye. He worked on one side, his handler on the other. Between them they guided the unmarked sheep off in ones and twos, allowed others to drift across—and all the time the two little flocks faced each other across the line between man and dog.

We who watched these two performances counted ourselves privileged. The one regret is that we may recapture them in memory only and not on cine. We may not see their like again. The shedding ring for National trials is marked in sawdust. It is now forty yards in diameter, an absolutely ludicrous size. You feel that you are in a twelve-acre field, and might get lost in it. A marked ring is a good idea, but I think it should only be a guide. To penalise a man if he is a foot over the ring causes friction, and seems pointless; it is not practical shepherding.

The shepherd must help his dog with stick or hand. With some sheep the dog must keep its distance; with others it may work tight. In my opinion, to complete the shed the man may step forward one pace provided that the dog comes through in the proper manner. It is no use if the man runs in to separate the sheep and then asks the dog to join him. Sheep will often reunite if the dog does not come through smartly enough.

For most men and most circumstances it is essential to keep the sheep quiet while shedding. When Ken won the English National at Blackpool, one of the unmarked sheep was the wildest imaginable. The only possible course was to take the other two, and with a dog like Ken you could do that sort of thing. Ken ignored the awkward sheep. He didn't try to turn it or put pressure on. Had he done so, it would have been off like a rocket. Eventually he got the other two off, leaving the trouble-maker behind.

Things do not always work out so well. In the Supreme at Beaumaris, Anglesey, Snip had to shed five ribboned sheep out of twenty. Of the fifteen unmarked sheep, thirteen had been taken but one ribboned sheep tried constantly to run away. As a last resort, for I was getting desperate for time, I let Snip turn it a bit sharp, but it never settled again. We got one off, but not the other, thus failing to complete the shed. According to the International Sheep Dog Society no points are allowed for the shed if incomplete. In my opinion a man and dog who set about their task in workmanlike fashion, shedding off all except the last one or two sheep, deserve more than a pair who dashed the sheep about and had hardly started shedding.

If, on completion of the shed, those sheep you have let go have run some distance away, it is necessary to fetch them back and reunite them with the others. As soon as circumstances permit, move towards the pen yourself. Having reached it, start to think about getting the sheep to the pen mouth and, unless you have complete faith in your dog, keep an eye on what is happening. I have seen men stroll casually to the pen while a young dog behind lets slip one of its sheep. The way the sheep approach the pen is very important. Stand well back, as far as your rope will allow, as they come near, and try to get them right to the pen mouth before making any move. Some people try to pen before all the sheep have arrived, and in effect push them round the pen instead of allowing the proper approach. If time is running out you may try to force them in, but nine times out of ten you fail.

A common occurrence is a sheep 'bursting' at the pen. The reason is that the dog has pressed too hard before the sheep are ready for pressing. If a sheep has broken once, it is liable to keep on doing so. Your chief objective is to maintain a quiet approach. If the sheep simply stand without moving, it is to be hoped your collie has power to walk right up, full of confidence. Some excellent penning dogs simply move their head and shoulders, and not their feet; with a confident collie this may be enough. Positioning is all-important.

International Sheep Dog Society rules state that:

> The pen will be six feet by nine feet with a gate six feet wide to which is secured a rope six feet long. On completion of shedding the handler must proceed to the pen, leaving his dog to drive the sheep to the pen. The handler is forbidden to assist the dog to drive the sheep to the pen. The handler will stand at the gate holding the rope and must not let go of the rope while the dog works the sheep into the pen. The handler will close the gate. After releasing the sheep, the handler will close and fasten the gate.

This done, he proceeds to the shedding ring, leaving the dog to bring the sheep. In the Nationals, two of the five sheep are ribboned, and one of these has to be shed off. This is the single. While singling, all sheep must be inside the shedding ring, and the sheep shed off inside the ring. Thereafter the sheep is worn (kept away from the others) to the judges' satisfaction, inside or outside the ring, and the judges shout, 'That will do!' At other trials it may be that the last sheep has to be singled, which is more difficult than shedding one of two marked sheep at the National.

The principle of singling when at work, as outlined in Chapter 8, applies equally on the trials field, as of course it should, as trials are a more precise extension of farm working conditions. At a small trial the handler must remove his own sheep after completion, but at National and International level there are volunteer handlers to do this, and their willing collies often intrigue the crowd as much as do the competitors.

Town and country audiences alike love to see the doubles run, with two dogs working at the same time. The handler's first essential is a pair of compatible collies. They must nick in with one another and not be jealous. I should amplify this by stressing that they must not be jealous while working, for my present pair, Cap and Roy, are as jealous as can be of one another once the job is finished. Roy doesn't like Cap coming near me—he is protecting me in his way, standing at my feet and keeping Cap off. Yet at work this doesn't show. I once tried to double with a brother and sister pair, Don and Snip. They were quite incompatible. Don was very strong, and needed such continual commands that Snip was quite upset. Things got so bad that I retired before completing the cross-drive.

The next point is to have two dogs on different commands. This is not absolutely essential, but it makes doubling very much easier. We assume that these basics are available, and that the run is about to start. Go to your starting stake, setting one dog down on one side, and its mate on the other. It is very nice if both dogs can start together, but this is not always possible. The real aim is to have them finishing their outrun together, and to achieve this the handler must take several factors into consideration. One dog may be slower than the other, in which case it must set off first. Natural obstacles may make the probable outrun longer on one side than the other, or the sheep may have already started to wander to one side.

The gather is exactly the same as in singles events. International Sheep Dog Society rules permit the dogs to cross behind their sheep on the gather, but having done so, they must stay to that side. If they cross again, they are wrong. I don't practise this; my dogs stay as they are sent, and it seems natural to them to pull in together.

Doubling is not working first one dog and then the other. Both work the sheep at the same time. At the start, it is possible that one collie arrives before the other, and that the sheep drift away, but its companion should be brought into station as soon as possible. The course is similar to the singles, with twice the number of sheep. When turning corners, have one dog slightly in advance of the other.

Once round the corner, each dog takes up its driving position at the angle of the flock. When passing through the drive obstacles, one collie goes further than the other, then lines up for position straight across the field. With two sets of whistles it is possible to work away quite steadily, but when I was a lad the dogs had to stop and wait until their name was called. Turning for home round the second cross-drive obstacle a tight corner is again the aim, followed by a steady and straight line to the shedding ring.

Here the flock must be split into two equal groups. To do this, both dogs may be in front, ie on the opposite side of the sheep from the handler, or one in front (dog 1) and one behind (dog 2). I prefer the latter method. Having prepared a suitable gap, ask the dog in front to come through, turning those sheep nearer to the first pen away from the others. Then bring dog 2 on to the sheep you are dispensing with, directing it to take them away to a safe distance. This should be just far enough to ensure that

93

there is no danger of them affecting or joining up with the other sheep. Leave dog 2 to guard them, so that it continues to hold its sheep away from you and its partner.

The handler now proceeds to Pen 1, directing dog 1 to bring its sheep to the pen. Penning is similar to that described in singles running, except that the pen has no gate or rope. This makes it more difficult, as the gate helps to a surprising degree. The shepherd stands at one side of the sheep and the dog at the other, both penning, just as they would if at work.

Once in the pen, bring the collie to the front. Its task is now to hold the sheep in, unaided and without further commands. If the sheep are of a wild nature, place your dog further back—say one and a half yards from the pen mouth—than if the sheep are placid. Set the dog squarely across the pen mouth, so that the sheep see the whole of the dog all the time. Most Border collies lie willingly, but Ivor Hadfield's Ben always stood. He quivered as though he was about to set off any second, but never did. Ben must have stood guard for hours; he and Tip made a great doubles pair. A properly disciplined dog usually has no great difficulty in learning that it must stay. For training, I take two dogs and one lot of sheep, making each dog in turn lie down and stay down while the other is working. Seeing another collie working causes the greatest temptations.

Now proceed to the second pen. Dog 2 has to gather up its sheep and bring them to the pen in the same manner as described for Pen 1. If you have difficulty, don't on any account let this second lot of sheep too near those in Pen 1, or they will try to join up, in which case you start all over again. During this second penning keep one eye looking over your shoulder to check that all is well at Pen 1. I well remember J. M. Wilson years ago, before my own trialling days, trying to pen his second lot before a big audience at Rydal in the Lake District. His first dog left its pen and was quietly crossing the field to help its pal. He was so intent on penning that he didn't notice this, till murmurings from the crowd reached his ears. He looked up, and there was his first dog within a few yards of him. I can't tell you what he said;

it was either Scotch or Gaelic—it certainly wasn't English—but that dog returned to its duties like a rocket, and didn't move again.

Having completed your second penning, you have finished your doubles run. One important point remains. Let out the sheep from Pen 2 as soon as they are penned satisfactorily, but don't call your dog from Pen 1 from a distance. Go over to it, then take it round to the back to drive the sheep out. This is sound and almost universal practice among doubles men; if it is not followed, the dog may decide on some other occasion that the time is up when in fact it isn't.

10

JUDGING

Be thou diligent to know the state of thy flocks.

Proverbs 27, v 23

The human element enters into trials judging. Too much so, in
my opinion, and this chapter is an attempt to standardise
methods and enlarge on the rules laid down by the International
Sheep Dog Society as I see them. ISDS lay down a standard of
points for National and International events. The difficulty is to
persuade judges to apply them in the manner intended. In the
American system, which I have not seen in operation, points are
assessed almost solely on success or otherwise of getting through

the various obstacles. A child could judge them. Yet to my mind this defeats the whole object of trials, which is to simulate working conditions and sort out dogs and handlers who bring sheep under steady, quiet control throughout.

The scale of points for a National singles championship is: Outrun 20; Lifting 10; Fetching 20; Driving 20; Shedding 10; Penning 10; Single 10; total 100 points. Time limit 15 minutes, no extension.

Judging and timing start from the moment the dog sets off for its sheep. Though no points are deducted as the man walks to the stake, I like to note how his dog behaves at this stage. It should accompany him quietly to the post, stand and look upfield, and a seasoned dog should indicate immediately it has seen the sheep by standing tense, with ears cocked. A dog should not be peeping about all over the place, or wandering. If it is not under full command at this early stage, look out for trouble later, but no markings are made on the sheet. All trials are judged by deducting marks for faults, not by adding good points. Pen and paper are needed, and specially designed score-sheets are obtainable from Matt Mundell, *Scottish Sheepdog Handler*, 23 Abercrombie Road, Castle Douglas, Scotland.

The outrun is the first and very important stage. Its course should be pear-shaped, gradually opening up as the dog goes on its way. Any dog that spins round before setting off should be penalised. As it passes level with the sheep, it should be at its greatest distance from them. Imagine the course as a clock, with the waiting sheep at the centre; the dog is level with the sheep at 3 o'clock or 9 o'clock, according to whether it is a left-hand or right-hand run. After reaching this point the collie completes the pear shape by turning in towards its sheep, and ends its outrun at 12 o'clock if the sheep are in position and facing downfield towards the handler. This is an ideal that seldom happens. The sheep may have turned away from the handler and be facing the dog. In this case the dog should pull up when it is facing them, even if only at 1 o'clock on a right-hand run. If the sheep have wandered away to the handler's left on a right-hand run, the dog must go past them—to 11 o'clock. In any event the object is for dog, sheep and first obstacle to be in a direct line.

It is not essential for the dog to stop dead at the end of the outrun, nor for the handler to whistle it down. The outrun is concluded perfectly satisfactorily if the dog merely slows down in the correct position; if it has gone too far, or not far enough, points must be deducted. A dog that needs further commands to take it to its place should be penalised compared with one that ends the outrun correctly of its own volition. Other penalties are imposed for stopping on the outrun, for looking back at its handler instead of keeping its eyes on the sheep, and for crossing its course. That is a big fault, which I define as crossing right over in front of the sheep and starting to gather them from the opposite side to which it set off. For this fault I would deduct three-quarters of the outrun points. If a dog merely crosses the centre line and then runs back to its correct side, that is much less serious. Dogs which need redirection commands on the outrun, to 'blow' them wider or, less frequently, tighter, must receive a slight penalty, as they are obviously less effective than a dog that sets a perfect course without commands. Also, a dog that responds immediately by swinging in or out is penalised far less than one that sails on regardless!

The outrun ends when the dog stops or slows down behind its sheep. The 'lift' follows. In a proper lift the sheep's heads come up and they drift away from the dog. Once the sheep are under way, the lift ends. It takes very little time, but it is important, for their initial reaction to the dog affects the sheep's subsequent behaviour. Ten points are at stake. Faults in a lift are when the dog has to be constantly called on to its sheep; if it must be stopped frequently on the way; and if it jumps in and upsets the flock. If a dog tears round the course at the end of its outrun, and sets off the sheep without slowing, deduct points from both outrun and lift. There are handlers who contend that a dog should stop at 12 o'clock on its outrun regardless of where the sheep are, and then move into position behind them. This is impractical, as is the practice of bringing sheep that are out of line when lifted back to where they should have been instead of taking them straight to the first obstacle. When shepherding you don't go round two sides of a triangle if you can go straight across. Other handlers contend that a dog that jumps in on the lift is 'strong'. I say the opposite; the dog should advance on the sheep steadily and without flinching.

Judges have been known to say that if the sheep have moved away from the post where they were released, the dog cannot have full points. This is wrong. We are judging the dog, not the sheep. The dog reacts to a situation that occurs constantly in everyday shepherding, and must deal with it accordingly. Similarly in the fetch, the dog may work well to one side of the sheep, because it must in order to keep them in line. Provided the sheep's course is true, the dog should not lose points for its own position. The fetch should be in a straight line to the first obstacle, and thence to the handler's stake. Having started the fetch, the sheep should be brought on steadily, without stopping to look round at the dog, to graze, or to break into a mad gallop. Some dogs work well up to their sheep, others command equally well by hanging back, but a judge should not class one superior to the other. A great deal of whistling during the fetch is not to be desired. It may be over-commanding, which leads to loss of points. Although the behaviour of the sheep must be taken into consideration, I would also deduct points if the dog had been putting on too much pressure and set the sheep galloping; if the sheep were gaining speed through the dog working too fast; and if they were looking round because the dog was too far away or too slow. Remember that there is a difference between a dog given to excessive 'clapping' or lying down, and one that must be frequently stopped to prevent it working too close. Provided the latter responds, you know that here is a dog capable of working sheep.

In the fetch the sheep's faces should be towards the judge throughout. They should pass tight up to the handler's stake, but it is no detriment if he moves a yard or two sideways to help his dog; he isn't a statue.

99

Corners are there to be turned, so deduct marks if the sheep are squandered about all over the place when cornering. However, always take account of sheep's differing natures; some will be as wild as the hills whence they came, and move at a gallop whatever the dog does.

Once past the handler's feet, the sheep are on the drive. This should be a straight line from the man to the centre of the first obstacle. It is not correct to take the sheep to one side and then hook them back through the hurdles. The same general principles apply as in the fetch; sheep should not be looking back at the dog, or corkscrewing all over the place. Twenty points are allowed for the drive, and should be divided by allowing eight from the handler to passing through the first obstacle of the drive, depending on whether it is a right- or left-handed drive; eight from there to passing through the second obstacle; and four back to the handler.

If obstacles are missed, you must deduct points. Zigzags culminating in a manoeuvre through the hurdles must also be penalised, and watch the turns through the hurdles. A half moon is not good, the result perhaps of a dog flying too far off its sheep, a pointer to its training.

The cross-drive is difficult to judge. You may have walked the course beforehand, and noted certain natural features in line between the two obstacles of the cross-drive, but seldom can any such points be seen from the judging arena. I have known competitors scatter hen feathers to give them a line, but these are equally invisible at a distance! The sheep should be seen side-on during the cross-drive, and provided they are going steadily ahead, and pass through the hurdles, the judge cannot be too severe. Sometimes spectators square with the cross-drive will say that the handler had a bad line, when from the handler's and judge's position it looked in order. I have known judges put a line of pegs to mark the cross-drive, but if they can see them so can the handler.

The last stage of the drive is often neglected. Sheep and dog have passed either by or through the last obstacle, and must now return steadily and quietly to the handler, who may not step from his post to meet them until the sheep are in the shedding ring. This ring is now forty yards in diameter, very large in comparison with its former twenty yards for the Nationals. The rules state that two unmarked sheep are to be shed off and that the dog must be in control of these two otherwise the shed will not be deemed satisfactory. Judges will apply a suitable penalty when an opportunity to shed is missed or if the dog fails to come through when asked.

Points should also be deducted if the man does too much of the work or if the dog jumps in too quickly or on to the wrong sheep. Judges must note that the correct number of sheep are ribboned; in the Nationals three of the five sheep are unmarked, and two of them must be shed. In a correct shed, the sheep are kept quiet, and opened up to give the dog a chance to come through in the right place.

For shedding, ten points are allowed, but if a man does not complete his shed he gets no points. I think this is wrong. The handler who has worked quietly and efficiently and has shed all except one recalcitrant ewe and is then beaten by the clock, is surely worth more than a handler who has dashed the sheep all over the place and not shed any. In the first instance, the handler's punishment is to be barred from penning, heavy enough in itself. There is a further point on which I disagree with the society. In their rules for the International they state: ' "Cutting" is forbidden, and should this be done the judges will order the lot cut off to be re-joined with the others and shedding recommenced.' By 'cutting' is meant bringing the dog through the lot to cut off any number. We had an old rabbit dealer who unfailingly supplied regular meals. When asked by a customer how he managed to catch so many rabbits he replied: 'Any way I can, ma'am, any way I can!' It is much the same with shedding. The sheep should be got rid of any way you can.

After shedding, the sheep must be joined up again, except at the International, where bigger numbers are involved. The next stage is the pen. The handler must go to the pen and direct his dog to bring the sheep to him; if he helps to drive them, points should be deducted. After opening the gate, the handler holds the end of the rope attached to it, and 'may assist the dog, but over-assistance should be penalised as should unsteadiness, rashness, slackness or any other fault shown by the dog'. To these International Sheep Dog Society rules I would add penalties if a dog runs in and then turns away. A 'burst' at the pen is a common sight, with sheep charging round the pen. Some judges deduct a point every time a sheep circles the pen, but with only ten points to play with you are soon out of points if sheep break two or three times.

Gripping is most likely to occur either at the pen or the shed. If severe it leads to disqualification. It is far worse if a dog darts in and grips the rear or flank, for in some cases a ewe will charge head on to the dog, who knows that its job is to turn that sheep, and it cannot do so by turning tail. Sometimes sheep are really stubborn, and stand their ground as the dog advances. If it touches them on the nose it is right. In all this we must never lose sight of what we require from a practical working dog. There is a world of difference between a dog that dashes a flock madly here and there, and one that refuses to give best to a ewe with its head down.

If sheep are settled outside the pen, refusing to move, there is no point in penalising a dog that decides to wait a while. It knows that if it puts on too much pressure the sheep will break, and that undoubtedly entails loss of points. I once lost a trial by pushing against the clock; the Swaledales concerned were almost in, and I tried to hurry them. One shot out, and judge Frank Tarn had no option but to dock my points and lose me first prize. A dog may have to back away and then advance to persuade the sheep. This should not be penalised; it is very different from turning tail.

Penning is completed when the gate is shut. In the brace, it is completed when man and dog are in front of the pen mouth, for had there been a gate they could have closed it. Then (in the single) the sheep are released. 'After releasing the sheep, the handler will close and fasten the gate,' say the rules, but they don't say what happens if this is not done. When Mr Harry Halsall was secretary, Captain MacPherson hurriedly completed his penning, glanced at his stop-watch, and dashed away without shutting the gate. 'Shut the gate!' called the secretary. 'If you want the gate shutting, ye shut it man. Ye've more time than me!' responded Captain MacPherson. Another Harry Halsall story concerned my brother Tot, whose young dog slipped on to the field when another handler was whistling. 'That man's disqualified!' said the secretary. And Tot was. There were no committee appeals in those days.

After penning comes singling. The most spectacular way is to stop the last sheep and let the others walk on. Generally a ribboned sheep has to be singled, or in a small trial the instruction may be to stop the last sheep. I would penalise a dog that needed two yards of room to cut off a sheep. A good singling or shedding dog comes through the smallest space. Roy lost me £25 at Keswick through doing just that. 'Come on, boss,' he indicated. 'Here's a sheep on its own. We must be having it!' But it was the wrong sheep! We were then placed equal with Glyn Jones and Gel, a Supreme pair, and Glyn won on faster time.

In doubles or brace running, each dog should converge on the sheep at the same time. They are allowed to cross behind the sheep at the conclusion of the outrun, but after that they must remain at their respective sides. Each must take its corner, and work accordingly. You are judging a brace run, not a single course with another dog on the field, so a perfect fetch with one dog doing all the work wouldn't satisfy me. Otherwise the same principles outlined for judging the single, fetch and drive apply.

Penning is different. Open pens are used in the brace, each dog penning his own after the sheep have been shed into two equal lots. Remember that there is no necessity to pen first with the dog used for shedding. The first lot is penned with one dog, who then stays on guard. If its sheep escape before the other has penned, the handler must come back and retrieve the error.

Once I was judging the English National at Cottesbrook, where my brother Tot was running Lad and Gyp. He penned with Gyp, who lay there conscientiously enough, but a sheep had such confidence in the dog that it started coming out to graze, with head and shoulders fully beyond the pen. Gyp did not move. If she had backed away she would have lost points, for the sheep would have come out, and Lad completed his job before any general escape occurred.

In driving competitions, the judge must look for such power in the dog that the sheep are being driven straight away from it. They must be packed throughout. Ringing—completely encircling the flock—is serious. The dog must work from one rear corner to the other, all the time forcing the sheep forwards and inwards. Once they become spread out a single dog's task is almost hopeless. Driving championships are largely confined to the International, where the dog representing each country has fifty sheep.

Judges are sometimes asked for reruns. Be very careful here. Only in very exceptional circumstances should such an appeal be upheld. A man can do things on purpose which make the sheep appear at fault. A ewe may drop down with her tongue hanging out, but before you decide she was unfit at the start, conjure up the dog's performance, and decide whether that sheep has been dogged into the ground.

Occasionally the pen-men make a mistake and let out the wrong number of sheep, or forget to ribbon them. When this happens, and the run is already under way before it is noticed, let things continue as long as possible. For instance, if the ribbons are absent, there is no reason to stop the dog until it reaches the shedding ring, because for fetch and drive the ribbons do not matter. Only then should the sheep be replaced.

OBEDIENCE AND WORKING TRIALS

Audrey Wickham

Upwards of a hundred years ago the breed as it then existed bore the highest reputation for intelligence and docility. The then Duke of Richmond was not above crossing one of his famous Gordon setters with a black-and-white Collie bitch, the property of a well-known poacher, with the object of improving the intelligence of his dogs.
        Standard Cyclopaedia of Modern Agriculture
                    (early twentieth century)

A horse trained in dressage does not require its skills under the practical conditions obtaining today, and the same applies to the finer points of dog obedience work. Yet dressage is accepted as very worthwhile in the horse world; obedience tests are regarded by some dog people as being rather far-fetched.

One very useful side of obedience training concerns the pet owners. Their participation forms the bread and butter of most clubs concerned with obedience and working trials. 'Pet people' want to train their dogs to walk tidily on a lead without constant tugging, to come when called and to 'Stay'. The dogs must not jump up, and retrieving is not expected. Once bitten by the obedience bug, however, pet owners frequently wish to carry training a stage further, and enter competitions.

There are now great numbers of these. Most of the year there may be eight obedience shows every Saturday, often with 300 entries and sometimes a thousand. For every dog attending a show, probably six to twelve pets are being trained for good manners. I cannot think of a better way of spending a Saturday than testing the abilities of my dogs against other people's dogs.

The Border collie is a very popular obedience dog. It is quick to respond, shows great willingness to please, has quick reactions and is bred to be trained. It is swift, easy to care for, and not too big. It also has disadvantages; Border collies are not really suitable pets, and obedience dogs tend to find themselves in a pet environment. One must be very careful with breeding lines, as some are a bit too effervescent for the home and the constrained nature of obedience competitions, while others are too hard. Often a good obedience dog is a good sheep dog; a sheep dog is of no use if it doesn't take orders. I usually have a dozen or so Border collies, and at least ten of them could work sheep. It is a great shame to breed Border collies simply for obedience, as some do. On the other hand, a shepherd is equally mistaken when he says to obedience people: 'This dog is no good to train with sheep, but it will be all right for your game!'

Obedience competitions are divided into five classes; Beginners, Novice, A, B and C. The first two comprise heel work on and off the lead, Recall, Retrieve and 'Stay' exercises. In these first two categories, any amount of encouragement is allowed. There is also a temperament test in the Novice class and class A, the dog standing beside its handler on a lead. The judge comes up and runs his hand down the dog's back. The dog must not shy away or show any sign of nastiness. It is a simple test, but it sorts out very temperamental dogs.

When the dog has worked well in the two novice classes, and not before, it is entered for class A. The number of commands allowed is cut down drastically, a Scent test is introduced, and recall is made more difficult. The handler's scent is on an article supplied by the handler and thrown among a lot supplied by the judge. In class B even fewer commands are given. There are different speeds in heel work, and heel work is done without a lead. Judge's articles are used for both retrieve and scent, and the dog must also do a Send-away and drop on command. Class C is far more complicated. The send-aways are usually more tricky. Heel work is done at three speeds and with three positions; the dog is left at stand, sit or down, the handler continuing without pause. There is distance control with no extra commands, a two minutes sit, and a ten minutes down with the dog out of sight of the handler. These seem fairly advanced, but the great stumbling block is the scent test, in which the dog must find a cloth with the judge's scent among other cloths. A square of cloth about the size of a lady's handkerchief is the usual article for testing scent. Yet recently there were ninety-seven dog competitors in a championship C class, and over eighty in the bitch class. So high is the standard that 290 points out of 300 are needed three times, before a dog is eligible for class C at a championship show.

Working trials are more practical. There are five stakes, starting with Companion Dog (CD). Other stakes are Utility Dog (UD), Working Dog (WD), finally rising to either Tracking (TD) or Police Dog (PD). In all these, obedience standards are not as high as in obedience competitions. A Companion Dog must have basic obedience, however, as in novice class obedience tests, and the send-away and an area search for one article. It must prove its agility with three jumps; 3ft scale, 9ft long-jump and 3ft clear-jump.

Tracking and steadiness to gunshot are introduced into Utility Stakes. The dog is required to follow a track of men's footprints half an hour old, with one article on the track to find or indicate. The area search is over a bigger space, and has four hidden articles. In working dog stakes the track is one and a half hours old and has two articles on it. There is a four-article area search in all tracking stakes. In Tracking Dog stakes a track three hours old is required, with three articles on it. On the send-away the dog is redirected after fifty or a hundred yards, as asked by the judge, and must also speak on command. This is virtually impossible with some Border collies. Mine seldom speak even when the rest of the kennels are in uproar because of some new visitors! However, only five points are at stake, and a Border collie may well be able to forfeit them and still qualify.

Border collies are seldom used for the grade parallel to tracking dog, which is police dog. They simply are generally not big and heavy enough, though Border collies are now being tried for scenting drugs. In Police Dog stakes the track is only half an hour old, but the dog must complete the 'man-work' tests. The dog must search for a criminal in a large area, bay and not attack when he is found, and hold him while the handler searches. The dog must be ready to defend its handler, and to prevent the escape of the criminal by running in and biting. It must stand up to a stick attack, and the technique is to go in and hold the forearm. In stick training the dog is not actually beaten; it is threatened with the stick and taught how to cope with it. A difficult part to this grade is the recall—to return immediately to heel when in full pursuit of a criminal, presumably the wrong one.

How does one choose a Border collie for Obedience or Working trials? It is important to start at the puppy stage, as contact with the handler is usually much closer than with sheep dogs. I choose a pup that responds; it wags its tail when spoken to, and comes to you. The pup is best brought up in the house, and played with a lot, especially with the hands. Do not use a choke collar. Training should not start too early, though the pup may be taught to 'Go to bed' and to drop on command at four to six months. House training is of course taught as with any puppy.

Encourage the pup to come when called, and make a fuss of it when it does. Shepherds seldom have much trouble with this, but a lot of the 'pet owners' tend to become cross when their pup does not come immediately, and of course next time it is worse.

Serious training depends on the dog. A 'tough' or hard dog may start at seven or eight months, a sensitive one may be twice that age. Remember the tremendous difference between individual Border collies, which seems to have become accentuated through breeding for sheep dog trials. Heel work is best taught free, or with a flat leather collar; never with a choke collar, except in the case of a very tough dog. Once a dog has experienced the choke collar, the memory takes months to erase. Far better teach the dog to want to please you, to watch and listen, than to do as it is told unwillingly. This is why my dogs work with their tails wagging!

The retrieve can be taught by various methods, using a dumb-bell, as we call the object to be retrieved. If possible, I develop this trait through playing with sticks and toys; keep it fun or the dog will go off.

The recall is important. The dog should come willingly, probably jumping up, and the handler moves back slightly, whereon the dog can be brought into the 'Sit' position in front. To begin, these exercises are done from a short distance, but later from greater lengths.

Practice is needed for all exercises. For training the 'Sit stay' and 'Down stay', the dog should be wearing a leather collar, and on the command 'Down' should be pressed down, held for a few seconds, and released by command or signal. I tap-tap on the dog's side for release. If the pupil starts to move, put your hand back in its collar and press down. It is most important that the dog does not move until given the signal. Border collies are natural at the drop. A dog can save its life by dropping on command.

For 'Sit', put one hand on the dog's chest and the other on the rump, and press into the required position. If the dog starts to move, always go back to the beginning.

Don't teach 'Stay' and recall in the same session, and when teaching retrieve I break off all other training, then go back to it all together. All exercises have a finish. The dog comes round the handler and sits on the left-hand side. To teach this from the sit-in-front position, the handler moves his right foot back, then forward, helping the dog to the correct position. In early stages, this is taught with a lead, later with hand signals.

When the dog is reaching a high standard in novice classes, start the send-away. To do this, set the dog down on some place you can recognise again—a patch of weeds or coloured grass. Move away, call the dog to you then send it back with a sweep of the arm. I can teach a Border collie to 'Go away' in ten minutes. Match voice with action. Persevere with this until the dog will go from ten paces, after which work up to any distance. If it falters start again. In most obedience competitions four little cups mark the spot where the entrant must go, though sometimes it is marked by a mat, a wooden pole or even a capstan!

Always indicate to the dog that you are about to do a send-away, or it will think it is on heel work. A hedge, or better still a wall, helps to teach redirection. Put the dog between yourself and the wall, a few paces distant. Send it to the wall, and then in one direction or the other, close up to the obstruction. If it walks towards you, force it back by going in yourself, scolding, and redirecting.

To teach scent, use anything other than the dumb-bell kept for retrieve. An old sock does very well. Let the dog smell it, then throw it away among various other articles, letting your dog see the throw. When sent to retrieve its nose goes down straight away; I have never yet known one that didn't, providing it is doing a good retrieve first. Once the dog has started to use its nose, you may pass on to more complicated scent patterns and more difficult articles.

There is only a limited amount of time for training. Dogs are not so easy to train after about three years old, and the work is as concentrated as training Border collies as sheep dogs—but you don't need sheep or space! Lots of obedience work is done indoors. I think training is often overdone. My usual schedule with a new dog is two weeks of 'Heel' and 'Stay', two weeks of retrieve and two weeks of both. Then ease right off, warming up just before a show. Once showing has started, my dogs do about twenty minutes per week, no more.

If it is intended to teach a dog to track, begin at about nine months. Do not teach to jump too young, as the joints may be damaged. In fact, for this, an eighteen-inch barrier serves—just high enough to make the dog jump to cross it. I go over the jump with them to start with, saying 'Over'. Say 'Over' again in a different key on the return, or use another word. To say 'Back' is not good, as this is needed in other situations. I use 'Amber', but the word does not matter provided it is consistent. Once a certain competence is reached, go on polishing up exercises, but not too often or for too long.

THE INTERNATIONAL SHEEP DOG
SOCIETY

*Hill farming and sheep dogs are linked because, like the plough
and a pair of horses, one is not much use without the other. But
whereas in ploughing operations, horses have been largely
dispensed with, in hill farming the sheep dog is indispensable
and must remain so.*

G. Lionel Pennefather
(former Irish National Champion)

Following the first sheep dog trials at Rhiwlas, Bala, in 1873,
more trials were held in Wales. Their popularity spread to other
parts of Britain, and were formalised by the founding of the
International Sheep Dog Society at Haddington in 1906.
Scottish enthusiasts were responsible, and the list of early
winners before World War I is dominated by Northumberland
and the Borders. Of the first nine Internationals, Scotland won
five, England four. Northumberland warrants special mention,
for early trials were staged at Otterburn.

After World War I the society resumed its work with no office bearers, no members, and a credit balance of £5. A stud book was founded, and trials were reformed. Today the society has 5,000 members with some 5,500 Border collies registered annually at the society's offices, St Andrew's House, Haughton Road, Darlington, Co Durham, Tel Darlington 52647.

In discussing the utility of sheep dog trials, we cannot better the words of former ISDS Secretary Mr James A. Reid in 1935.

What are the cumulative effects of all these factors of selective breeding and specialised training resulting from trials? It is our considered judgement that the breed stands today infinitely higher in working merit, and therefore in value, than ever it did. There is one decisive test. How comes it that the 'trial-bred' Collie of today has practically ousted the 'old-fashioned' Collie, and is ousting other breeds everywhere, eg the Old Welsh Sheep Dog? How comes it that he, with fleet limbs, eager eyes and ears, and lolling tongue, is found toiling silently, day in and day out all the year round, in every pastoral area of the British Isles? And how comes it that his or her sons and daughters are similarly labouring in foreign lands—in far-away Australia, the land of infinite distances, amid the towering mountains and valleys of New Zealand and Tasmania; on the vast rolling plains of Canada, and the never-ending sheep ranches of America, North and South; in the boundless spaces of the South African veldt, the Highlands of progressive Japan, and amid the cold fogs of the ocean-girt Falkland Isles? To these pregnant questions, the world-wide certificate of working merit, which fifty testing years of *performance* have given to our brilliant, brainy trial-bred Collies, is the conclusive answer.

Had James Reid lived to see the first world-wide Internationals, he would have been delighted but not surprised at the results. At Delaware, USA, against unfamiliar rules and course, four of the first five places were won by British handlers, Raymond Macpherson and John Templeton.

Britain's Supreme Championship came to be known as the Blue Riband of the Heather. It is popular television material, and Shep, bred by Audrey Wickham, is well known to millions of viewers of the children's TV programme, 'Blue Peter'. All this is a far cry from the days of James Hogg, the Ettrick shepherd, born 1770.

Early in the last century the collie was known in name and breed, though the exact meaning of the word is disputed. Rev E. B. Wallace in 1837 likened the value of a good sheep dog to the store farmer to the value of the threshing machine to the arable farmer, or the steam engine to the manufacturer. In the late eighteenth century great gatherings of men were needed to round up sheep, according to Wallace, and the next big step forward after the general adoption of the collie in their stead took place late in the nineteenth century. A good deal of shouting had accompanied dog work until a young Scottish shepherd, also named Wallace, gave the first recorded display of quiet working.

> By an almost inaudible hiss they (the Collies) dropped to the ground as if a bullet had passed through their brains. This style of handling was a revelation and a wonder to all who had the good fortune to witness it.

Since then, basic facts about sheep dog training have become part of the shepherd's life. He knows, as James Reid said, that before he can expect to train a dog to the highest pitch, he must discipline himself in patience, temper, and other necessary qualifications. And he must study dog character.

Today letters arrive at the International Sheep Dog Society office from all over the world, seeking information on pedigrees, trials results, and where to buy a well-bred Border collie. It is for this reason that any attempts to hold show classes for the breed are to be deplored, unless they are linked to working abilities. Sometimes, at the end of a trial, prizes are given for the best-looking dog, which must either have run in the trial or belong to a member of the local sheep dog association. This is just to add interest to a sociable afternoon, and to encourage youngsters to take care with the grooming of their charges. It has no connection whatever with current attempts to establish show standards for the Border collie in which height, coat, colour, set of ears and eye colour would be laid down. Such a move would do nothing but harm to the working collie and its potential export market as a working dog. A buyer in South Africa or Australia would feel less confident if he thought that another, non-working strain was being established in what to him is a very small country.

Enough has been written in this book to show that the best dogs have been of all colours, coats and sizes. There should be only one standard for the Border collie—work. It has been bred for generations by men whose own legs are saved by its performance. Let it remain that way.

GLOSSARY

Bad sheep: Uneven, ragged movers, liable to break at any moment, or turn and fight the dog. One individual may constantly seek to leave the rest. Sheep vary according to temperature, so may become worse during the heat of the day.

Doubles, brace running: Handler and two dogs working simultaneously.

Drive: The sheep go away from the handler, the dog behind them, usually steering a triangular course bounded by two pairs of hurdles through which the sheep should pass.

Ewe: Female sheep.

Fetch: After the lift, the sheep are driven towards the first obstacle, and usually towards the handler.

Gather: To collect sheep with a dog, in field or moor, from their scattered grazing positions into a compact mob.

Good sheep: In handlers' parlance, these are sheep that trot away nicely in front of the dog on the drive, remain in one flock, do not show fight and are all of equal stamina.

Heavy sheep: Sluggish and perhaps stubborn in movement. They allow a dog to work much closer to them than light or flighty sheep.

Hill, moor, fell: Names in different regions for large stretches of ground, usually rugged upland, which may have no fences or walls.

In-bye: Enclosed fields whose limited area makes sheep work easier.

ISDS: International Sheep Dog Society.

Lift: The period immediately after the dog has stopped at the extent of its outrun, before starting the sheep in intended direction. Important because it gives the sheep their first impression of the dog.

Light sheep: Opposite of heavy.

Outrun: Course taken by dog in gathering its sheep at a trial. Ideal course is pear-shaped, the handler being at the stalk of the pear and the sheep midway between the widest points.

Overshot jaw: The upper jaw is longer than the lower, consequently top and bottom teeth do not meet correctly. More a breeding than a working fault.

Pen: Small enclosure with or without a gate, into which sheep are driven without being touched by hand or dog, near conclusion of run.

Shed, shedding: Parting certain sheep from the rest. Larger trials usually include a shed.

Single, singling: One sheep, and one only, is separated from the rest and held off them by the dog.

Singles running: Handler and one dog.

Strong dog: All references to strength and power reflect solely on the dog's attitude to sheep. Nothing to do with physical characteristics. A strong dog comes up to its sheep, does not flinch if they attack it, and has a hidden power that dominates the sheep.

Strong eye: A dog which stares intently at its sheep, sometimes without moving. A characteristic bred in from gun dogs (setters). In extreme cases the dog spends its time on the ground and does not work the sheep. Less prevalent than formerly.

Tup: Ram, male sheep for breeding, usually of aggressive character.

Weak dog: Reverse of strong, above. Weak dogs turn tail if the sheep shows fight, work at the flanks of a small mob rather than at the centre. Lack power to work a large mob, though may win small trials on good sheep.

Wearing: When sheep are shed or singled, those held back are said to be 'worn' by the dog.

BIBLIOGRAPHY

Combe, Iris. *Collies Yesterday and Today* (Colchester, 1972)

Firbank, Thomas. *I Bought a Mountain* (1940)

Gossett, A. L. J. *Shepherds of Britain* (1911)

Grant, David & Hart, Edward. *Shepherds' Crooks and Walking Sticks* (Lancaster, 1972)

Hartley, C. W. G. *The Shepherd's Dogs* (Christchurch, New Zealand, 1949)

Herries McCulloch, J. *Sheep Dogs and Their Masters* (1938)

Holmes, John. *The Farmer's Dog* (1960)

Hudson, W. H. *A Shepherd's Life* (1910)

Kelley, R. B. *Sheep Dogs* (1942)

Moorhouse, Sydney. *The British Sheepdog* (1950)

Ollivant, Alfred. *Owd Bob* (1898)

Pennefather, G. L. *Sheepdogs*

Robertson, R. B. *Of Sheep and Men* (1960)

Many of the above are out of print, but may sometimes be found through antiquarian and country booksellers.

ACKNOWLEDGEMENTS

Acknowledgements to:

The International Sheep Dog Society
The Field
Penny Whaley who typed the manuscript

INDEX

Barking, 38, 59

'Beardie', 16, 41

Bitch, 16; feeding, 27; breeding, 30–3, 42

Biting, *see* gripping

Brace, 50, 53, 92–5, 102–3, 116

Breeding, 29–37

Buildings, 26, 28, 31

Cap, 5, 16, 30, 49, 62, 64, 70, 73, 92

Cattle, 15, 20, 21, 30

Certificate, 28

Check cord, 62–3

Collar, 59, 108, 109

Colour, 15, 16; choice of, 19; 29, 114

Command, commands, 20–1, 34, 44, 50–4, 59, 61–6, 68–9, 71, 73, 77–9, 82, 83, 85, 92, 97–9, 107–9

Cost, of buying, 23

Course director, 78, 82

Crook, *see* stick

Cross-drive, 86, 92–3, 100

Diseases, 27–8

Drive, driving, 12, 38–9, 49, 54, 64; teaching, 65–6, 67, 70, 71, 73; at trials, 85–7, 91; brace, 93, 96, 100; judging, 102–4

Ears, set of, 16, 29

Eye, 16; amount of, 20, 67–8

Feeds, feeding, 11, 23, 25–7, 31–2, 59

Fetch, the, 65, 71, 84–5, 97, 99–100, 103–4, 116

Fell, *see* hill

Folds, *see* yards

Gather, 19, 20, 23; reasons for, 38–40, 43–4, 64, 66, 71, 93, 116

'Go-back', 54; teaching, 68–71

Grip, gripping, 59, 67, 72, 102

Hill, worth in, 23, 38–44, 49, 68, 71, 72, 78, 88, 100, 112, 116

Housing, 26, 28, 31

Hurdle, 85–7, 100, *see also* obstacle

Innoculation, 27–8; of sheep, 41

International Sheep Dog Society, 16, 22, 29, 34, 78; rules of, 91, 93, 96, 101–2; formation and origins, 112–5, 117

International trials, 19, 21, 30, 79, 82, 84, 88

Jones, Alan, 37, 67, 89

Judge, judging, 77, 79, 82, 84, 92, 96–104, 106, 108

Ken, 5, 20, 21, 26, 31, 43, 60, 70, 85, 90

Kennel, 26, 28, 31, 56

Lambing, lambs, 21, 23, 39–43, 44, 49, 59, 74
Lead, leading, 56, 59, 106, 110
Lift, the, 84; description of, 97–9, 117
Longton, Tot, 31, 51, 79, 103, 104

Mating, 29–31; cost of, 31
Mature dog, *see* older

Nell, 5, 16, 26, 33, 34, 42, 49, 86; Hetherington's, 79
Novice class, 106–7, 110

Obedience, 12, 14; competitions, 106
Obstacle, 83–5, 87, 93, 96–100, 116; *see also* hurdle
Older dog, 16, 19, 21–3, 27, 60–1, 69–70, 72
Outrun, 39, 65, 82–3, 93, 97–8, 103, 117

Pen, penning, 12, 39, 44, 67, 71–2, 78, 89, 91, 93–5, 97, 99–104, 106, 108
Progressive retinal atrophy (PRA), 30
Punishment, 63
Pups, 16, 19, 22–3, 27–8, 31–3; training, 56, 59–62, 65, 73; for obedience, 108–9

Ram, *see* tups
Recall, 106, 109
Registration, 31
Rerun, 104
Retrieve, 106, 109–10
Richardson, John, 34, 60, 87
Roy, 5, 19, 33, 62, 73–4, 79, 92

Scent, 41, 107, 108, 110
Shearing, 43–4
Shed, 11, 20, 54, 66–7, 68, 69, 71, 88–92, 97, 101–3, 117
Shedding ring, 12, 87, 89, 90, 92, 93, 100, 104
Shows, showing, 106, 107, 111, 114
Singling, 66–7, 74, 92, 103, 117
Snip, 5, 26, 82, 90, 92
Snow, 41, 42
Stick, 42, 65, 90
'Strong' dog, 37, 49, 83, 99, 100, 104
Supreme championship, 34, 87, 89, 90, 103, 113

Tail, 16, 19, 33
Temper, 61, 74, 114
Temperament, 20, 33, 37, 106, 107
Tests, obedience, 106–11
Tracking, 41–2, 107–8, 111
Trials, 11, 12, 13, 19, 20, 28–33, 39, 40, 50–2, 60; nursery, 77–8, 79–104, 114, 117
Triangular drive, 86, 87, 100, 116
Tups, tupping, 19, 39, 40, 49, 60, 73, 117

Vaccine, *see* innoculations

Weak dog, 16, 20, 72, 83, 117
Whelping, 31–2
Whistles, 20–1, 50–3; plastic, 51, 62, 63, 66, 69, 70–1, 82, 83, 85, 93, 98–9, 103
Winter, 41–2

Yards, 12, 39, 44, 56, 71, 72